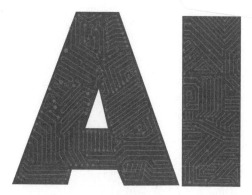

FOR
Small
Business

From Marketing and Sales to HR and Operations,
How to Employ the Power of Artificial Intelligence
for Small Business Success

Phil Pallen

ADAMS MEDIA
NEW YORK   AMSTERDAM/ANTWERP   LONDON   TORONTO   SYDNEY   NEW DELHI

Adams Media
An Imprint of Simon & Schuster, LLC
100 Technology Center Drive
Stoughton, Massachusetts 02072

First Adams Media trade paperback
edition January 2025

ADAMS MEDIA and colophon are
registered trademarks of Simon &
Schuster, LLC.

For information about special discounts
for bulk purchases, please contact Simon &
Schuster Special Sales at 1-866-506-1949
or business@simonandschuster.com.

The Simon & Schuster Speakers Bureau
can bring authors to your live event. For
more information or to book an event,
contact the Simon & Schuster Speakers
Bureau at 1-866-248-3049 or visit our
website at www.simonspeakers.com.

Interior design by Kellie Emery
Illustrations by Phil Pallen Collective
Images © 123RF/amisb

Manufactured in the United States of
America

1 2024
Library of Congress Cataloging-in-
Publication Data

Names: Pallen, Phil, author.
Title: AI for small business / Phil Pallen.
Description: First Adams Media
trade paperback edition. | Stoughton,
Massachusetts: Adams Media, [2025] |
Includes index.
Identifiers: LCCN 2024019294 |
ISBN 9781507222911 (pb) | ISBN
9781507222904 (ebook)
Subjects: LCSH: Small business--
Technological innovations. | Artificial
intelligence--Industrial applications. |
Technological innovations--Management.
Classification: LCC HD62.7 .P367 2024 |
DDC 658.02/2--dc23/eng/20240502
LC record available at
https://lccn.loc.gov/2024019294

ISBN 978-1-5072-2291-1
ISBN 978-1-5072-2290-4 (ebook)

Contents

Preface

Artificial intelligence (AI) moves at lightning speed, and it can feel impossible for small business owners to keep up. I should know—I am one!

Since 2020, I've shared my insights on AI and business on social media with a community of over two hundred thousand small business owners like yourself. I've shown how AI tools can help you automate tasks, save time and money, make more informed decisions, and grow your business faster. I've tested out literally hundreds of AI tools, and I've figured out which ones are worth your time and which ones are not. While I have existing relationships with some of the tools mentioned in this book—whether through creating sponsored content or earning from affiliate sales—none of them have paid to be included here. My aim is to only recommend tools that I've personally tried or thoroughly researched. My approach to AI is rooted in practicality; if it's too complicated for the average business owner to use or understand, then I won't recommend it.

Outside my social media community, I've worked with more than four hundred clients, ranging from budding entrepreneurs to *Fortune* 500 companies, through my branding agency. I've been on the front lines of the "AI overwhelm" for years, where business owners want to leverage AI to build the company of their dreams but don't know where to start. Through this book, I'm going to teach you everything I know—as a business owner, for business owners—so you have clarity on how to incorporate AI into your business functions.

Let's get started.

Introduction

The hype around AI makes the technology seem both exciting and a bit overwhelming. Those promises to save time and money sound intriguing, but how can you be sure AI will be a good match for your business? It can be a challenge to find the time to research how to implement AI for your company, when you have your hands full running that company in the first place! What you need is a practical guide that focuses on how AI can be leveraged for *your* needs without all the buzzwords and false promises.

Fortunately, *AI for Small Business* offers realistic strategies for utilizing this technology to help with your business's daily tasks—so you can spend more of your time growing your business! This book is both a road map *and* a how-to guide. In it you'll find information on building an AI strategy, ways to automate some of your daily operations, and inspiring stories about other small business owners who have discovered ways to make AI improve their workflows and their lives. But most importantly, you will discover how to harness AI's power to grow your business in all areas, including:

- Sales
- Marketing and Advertising
- Social Media and Content Creation
- Customer Service
- Finance and Accounting
- Operations and Logistics
- Human Resources and Talent Management
- Data Analysis and Decision-Making

- Security and Legal Compliance
- R&D and Innovation

With this book, you'll discover that AI *can* save you time and money. AI will help free you from the day-to-day drudge so you can apply your mind to creative pursuits. Think of this book as a primer—your life buoy in the choppy waters of AI technology, keeping you afloat so you can enjoy the process of exploring and adapting it for your business. You've got this! This book is here to guide you every step of the way.

PART 1

The chapters in this first part will help you dip your toe into the waters of artificial intelligence before discussing specific ways to utilize it in your business. Artificial intelligence can be overwhelming, so this part will help you get oriented with the landscape, allowing you to feel more familiar and confident with the technology before determining how to apply it to your small business.

By the end of these chapters, you'll have a solid understanding of artificial intelligence, including its definition and an overview of its intriguing history. You'll be well versed in the different types of machine learning—a crucial aspect of AI—and start to get glimmers of possible uses for your company. You'll also review artificial intelligence's ethical implications, including addressing some common (and understandable) causes for concern.

Once you have a lay of the land, you'll learn how to build a comprehensive artificial intelligence strategy for your business. You'll receive specific and easy steps to assess your business needs and tactics to identify opportunities to integrate artificial intelligence. You'll also go through a generative AI example exercise so that you can give ChatGPT, Gemini, Copilot, or Claude a spin.

Let's begin!

Chapter 1

Understanding the Basics of AI

Before you dive into the practical application of artificial intelligence, it's important to understand the basics and history of this technology. AI can be utilized in limitless ways for businesses, but its large scope can feel overwhelming, so a bit of background knowledge can help you feel more grounded and prepared. This chapter will discuss machine learning, natural language processing, and even some of the ethical concerns you may have about using AI. As a small business owner, you can benefit from the scientific and mathematical explorations that have been refined over the past decade, and you'll discover that using AI can improve your business practices and profits. Let's get started!

WHAT IS ARTIFICIAL INTELLIGENCE?

Artificial intelligence can be defined in a myriad of ways, but at its core, it combines computer science and datasets to solve problems. Artificial intelligence is, in essence, the confluence of human intelligence and computer science. AI can operate in a humanlike way—in writing, calculations, and research—with the rapid speed of computer processing. What is so amazing is how this emerging technology can be an unprecedented opportunity for entrepreneurs like you. With human guidance and supervision, AI can enact "human" tasks at a speed far faster than our brains can process and create many efficiencies for small businesses.

A BRIEF HISTORY OF ARTIFICIAL INTELLIGENCE

Artificial intelligence might seem new to the general public, but its origins date back to the seventeenth century, when philosophers, writers, and creative thinkers started to contemplate the idea of AI: What will happen when machines are able to harness human logic?

In the 1950s, society's technological and mathematical advancements allowed us to explore the inevitable possibility of artificial intelligence when renowned mathematician Alan Turing published a groundbreaking paper, "Computing Machinery and Intelligence," where he devised a test (the Turing test) to evaluate intelligent behavior and logic in machines.

Within six years of Turing's publication, the very first artificial intelligence program—the Logic Theorist—was created by Allen Newell, Cliff Shaw, and Herbert Simon. In a time when few households had computers, the Logic Theorist could prove complex mathematical theorems.

As decades passed, so did the advancements of artificial intelligence. From ELIZA, a natural language computer processor created in the 1960s, to Deep Blue, a chess-playing computer program that beat world chess champion and grand master Garry Kasparov in 1997, the answer to the question that creatives deliberated for centuries became clear: When machines harness human logic, tasks can be done quicker and, in some cases, better.

BASICS OF MACHINE LEARNING

You might have seen or heard the term *machine learning* in tandem with artificial intelligence. In its simplest definition, *machine learning* is the ability of AI to learn and improve performance through data, with and without a human presence. This differs from a traditional computer program that simply performs the function a programmer tells it to do. In other words, standard computer programs require ongoing programming (by a human) to improve their output, whereas machine learning allows AI to improve itself—without a human's explicit programming, maintenance, or aid.

In simple terms, machine learning is an important foundational layer of AI. It makes it possible that, when AI is used to carry out typical "human tasks," the output comes very close to the result that would be generated by a human. AI can do that by using an algorithm, which is a set of instructions or rules followed by a computer to solve a problem or perform a task. In machine learning, algorithms process data to learn patterns and make predictions. Think of them as the building blocks that enable AI to function effectively.

Types of Machine Learning

Let's explore the different types of machine learning:

- **Supervised learning:** This type of machine learning is rooted in the process of labeling datasets. You give AI data, along with the correct labels for that data, and it then learns to assign the right labels to new data. A label is a specific tag or value that describes the data point, and it guides the algorithm in making accurate predictions. As you give more and more guidance on labeling data, AI becomes more accurate. For example, when AI evaluates credit applications for businesses, it processes the past loan application history to determine whether a new applicant is a high-risk or a good potential client. This might involve providing the AI with historical data on loan outcomes, along with criteria that define high risk versus good credit (these would be the "labels"). The model would then learn these patterns and apply them to new applications. Labels guide AI by tagging data points, helping the algorithm learn to make accurate predictions. For instance, in an email dataset, labels like "spam" or "not spam" teach AI to classify new emails correctly. Similarly, in image recognition, labels such as "cat" or "dog" enable AI to identify and categorize animals in new images.
- **Unsupervised learning:** This type also involves evaluating and labeling datasets. The difference here is that models sift through unlabeled data without the prompt or guidance of humans. Unlabeled data refers to information that has not been categorized or tagged with specific labels or values. An example of this in business is when an AI tool is used to manage inventory; the algorithm

can observe sales data to pinpoint patterns and, as a result, better optimize stock levels—all without requiring any kind of programming from a human! So, for instance, you might upload several months of sales data, and the AI algorithm analyzes these numbers to deduce insights about inventory and sales patterns.

- **Reinforcement learning:** Humans often use trial and error when completing tasks or making decisions, and reinforcement learning follows a similar pattern. In this type of machine learning, the AI system tests and observes results to make predictions or decisions for future tasks. This type of machine learning is especially prevalent in dynamic pricing algorithms, where prices change automatically based on computer analysis of market conditions and consumer behavior. Reinforcement learning is an incredible tool for maximizing profit and is used by many companies today to have precision pricing.

NATURAL LANGUAGE PROCESSING IN AI

Natural language processing (NLP) is a field within AI that enables computers to understand and interact with human language. This field is both complex and fascinating, as it considers the context and semantics of written communication to perform functions. For example, early NLP applications included computerized spellcheck programs. Nowadays, AI can perform much more complicated language-based tasks that can help your business both analyze and write text.

Text Processing

In this form of NLP, language is analyzed and ultimately organized by AI to complete a function. One example is Brand24, which is what's called a "sentiment analysis tool." It combs through social media, blogs, forums, and more to uncover mentions of your business. It can then analyze the text it captures and tell if social media mentions (i.e., the sentiments people share) about your business are positive or negative.

Understanding

It's one thing for an AI tool to upload words, but comprehending those words is another. Understanding functions in NLP permits the algorithm to fathom both the meaning and context of the human language. NLP specifically focuses on enabling this comprehension to facilitate interactions and responses. An example of this is an AI chatbot for fielding customer service–related inquiries.

Generation

Particularly relevant to business owners, the generation function of NLP enables artificial intelligence to create—in the form of written language, diagrams, designs, and even voice—a response to your request. AI's ability to generate a summary or output and, critically, generate something we humans will understand is remarkable. Lokalise is a prime example of NLP generation in action—it can generate text in a new language while considering the nuances of that language.

USING AI TO ANALYZE IMAGES AND VIDEO

Artificial intelligence technology isn't limited to numerical data and language. It now includes "computer vision," which is a branch of AI that deals with gathering information from and reading text within images and videos. We use our eyes to take in visual information and our brains to process that information, and now computer vision does the same for AI.

Computer vision systems are used in countless industries to complement human eyes. In retail, computer vision supports inventory management by viewing shopper behaviors with products and identifying physical stock on shelves that the consumer will want to purchase. This includes checking to see if stock is available and in the right quantities. In security, this technology monitors unusual activity, such as unauthorized entries. For instance, a computer vision system installed at a secure facility can instantly detect and alert security personnel when someone attempts to breach a restricted area. Computer vision has even made its way to the medical industry to diagnose diseases by seeing things in MRIs and X-rays that are difficult to detect with the human eye.

Creating Operational Efficiencies

If your business has a physical store or warehouse or involves in-person interactions, you might find computer vision helpful in making your business processes more efficient. Every second counts in business, and ample opportunities exist to incorporate computer vision for increased efficiencies. Some examples include:

- AI can serve as a quality control, inspecting your products to ensure high quality without defects or irregularities.
- AI can swiftly digitize physical documents, such as print records or receipts, with minimal errors.
- AI can monitor your work environment to scan for potential hazards and ensure safety precautions are implemented and followed.
- AI can analyze customer movements and flow in your establishment—such as a restaurant—to improve your layout and reduce bottlenecks during peak hours.

Enhancing the Customer's Experience

Whether you're B2B (business to business) or B2C (business to consumer), customers are the lifeblood of any business. Computer vision creates incredible opportunities to enhance the overall customer experience in a variety of ways, including the ability to:

- Help people conveniently shop from their homes through virtual try-on features, where they can test out accessories, clothes, makeup, furniture, and more.
- Integrate technology into your cashier kiosks to quickly identify your customers and create a seamless and unique shopping experience. This technology functions similarly to Face ID—using facial recognition to authenticate customers efficiently and securely.
- Provide helpful information about your product on displays whenever a customer interacts with the item in your store, which can further influence their purchase decision. For example, customers can scan a QR code to access detailed product information, reviews,

or promotional offers, which can further influence their purchase decision.

- Ensure accessibility for all in your space by helping visually impaired customers get real-time information about their surroundings.

Next-Level Computer Vision Capabilities

Computer vision can do more than just look at images and videos. It can analyze what's happening in them to provide new insights about your business and customers, including:

- Determining the demographics of event attendees—both B2B and B2C—through cameras, so you can tailor your messaging and talking points accordingly. This might involve setting up cameras to capture people walking into venues like conferences or trade shows, then analyzing the footage to estimate age, gender, and other demographic information.
- Monitoring visual trends in social media to inform your marketing efforts.
- Observing the emotions in your customers' facial expressions to better understand what parts of their shopping experience create delight. This would mean placing cameras near your product displays to watch customers as they shop, capturing their facial expressions to gauge reactions.

As a business owner or operator, you may find computer vision to be a useful tool to make sense of your business's visual patterns. This technology ultimately helps to create efficiencies, better understand customers, and make smarter business decisions.

ROBOTICS PROCESS AUTOMATION

Another aspect of AI that is particularly useful for businesses is robotics process automation, or RPA. In essence, RPA is a feature of AI that can complete simple tasks over and over. Unlike humans who grow mentally fatigued with repetitive tasks, RPA technology can do repetitive tasks more efficiently with no errors or breaks. It's like an around-the-clock robotic assistant!

You can likely imagine the possibilities of using RPA to handle repetitive tasks within your business, but here are a few examples that might inspire you:

- For customer service, you can utilize RPA as an initial "customer service representative" that handles standard questions and follow-ups. Unlike NLP tools, which understand and generate human language, RPA focuses on automating repetitive, rule-based tasks without needing language comprehension. For example, RPA can automatically send follow-up emails based on preset rules, while an NLP tool can understand and respond to customer inquiries in natural language.
- RPA can handle all logistics for supply chain management precisely, including tracking orders and monitoring shipments.
- For human resources and hiring, RPA can rapidly review hundreds of resumes in order to identify the best candidates for your available positions.
- In finance, RPA can rapidly streamline bookkeeper duties, including data entering, transaction processing, and overall data management.

If your mind is spinning from all of the potential applications of AI, don't worry. Future chapters will help you create a strategy for gradually evaluating, testing, and onboarding AI into your business.

HOW TO USE GENERATIVE AI TOOLS

Generative AI platforms are used for inquiry purposes, meaning you can ask them questions and receive responses. This makes them different from other AI tools that might specialize in specific tasks like image recognition or predictive analytics. Generative AI tools are designed to understand and generate humanlike text based on the input they receive.

ChatGPT is a well-known option, but alternatives like Claude, Gemini, Magai, and Copilot also bring unique strengths to the table. For instance:

- Claude AI, developed by Anthropic, stands out with its clean interface and focus on safe, real-time assistance.
- Magai stands out by offering access to multiple AI models, including GPT platforms, providing users with the latest AI advancements in a simple interface.
- Google's Gemini feels familiar, like a Google search, offering an integrated way to double-check answers and provide sources.
- Microsoft's Copilot integrates deeply into the Microsoft ecosystem, excelling in coding assistance and task automation within Office applications.

Sometimes it simply comes down to personal preference when choosing among them. And you can even use AI to help you find the right AI tools! Get it?

How to Write Prompts

Generative AI tools can provide incredible answers when you request specific information or ask them questions. These requests are called "prompts." You can supply additional background information or data along with your prompt to give the tool personalized context for it to use as it works. Prompts can be long or short, casual or formal, and can even include attachments if you're using certain tools. Here's an example to show you what a prompt can look like.

When crafting prompts for generative AI tools, remember there's no definitive right or wrong way, despite what some say. Improvement comes with experience. Just like learning a new language, confidence builds with practice. Start with clear and specific questions to guide the AI effectively, and don't be afraid to experiment with different prompt styles. Providing relevant context can enhance the AI's responses, making them more personalized and accurate. For example, I often specify to ChatGPT which words I want it to *avoid*, such as "unlock," "unleash," or "game changing." Over time, you'll develop a knack for what works best for your needs. Don't let anyone put undue pressure on you by saying there's a definitive right or wrong way to craft prompts.

AI'S ETHICAL IMPLICATIONS FOR BUSINESS

Artificial intelligence is a tool that can help people, businesses, and communities thrive. However, some parts of AI can, understandably, cause concern from an ethical standpoint. Let's sort through these issues:

- **Isn't it risky to become overly dependent on technology?** This is a valid concern, but whether you like it or not, most businesses are already very dependent on technology. From my standpoint, AI is simply a natural progression of technology adoption in businesses. In fact, you might be unknowingly utilizing AI functions in your business already. The best advice here is to diversify the types of technology you adopt into your business practices and ensure that AI complements the human decision-makers in your organization.

- **Is collecting and analyzing videos and images of customers unethical?** We are in somewhat new territory regarding AI privacy laws and customers. A good rule is always to notify your customers when they're on camera or when collecting their data. A simple "you are on camera" sign at your store or an "unsubscribe" option in your email (both of which you should already have) should bring appropriate transparency to your customers.

- **Is using AI going to create job losses?** With any advancing technology, the job market will likely be impacted. However, research suggests that the outcome of AI isn't as bleak as it might seem. A recent study by Goldman Sachs suggests that, while 7% of jobs may be replaced by AI, 63% will be complemented, and 30% will remain unaffected. Think about the prospect of AI taking over mundane tasks that humans previously did as allowing for more time available for people to do valuable strategic and creative work. Instead of viewing AI as a job replacement, view it as a way to re-skill your existing team to work alongside AI.

- **Does using AI make your business vulnerable in terms of privacy and security?** As with other forms of technology, there are safeguards you can put in place to protect yourself and your business when using AI. It is recommended to use only AI tools with strong security credentials, such as encryption, robust data protection, and frequent security updates. Make sure you know how those AI tools handle any user data you provide. Do not upload copyrighted materials. As mentioned previously, it is an essential best practice to communicate to your customers about how you use their data to build and sustain trust.

LOOKING FORWARD WITH AI

Artificial intelligence has endless potential as a tool to supercharge your business. If your business is a sailboat, then AI is a GPS, getting you where you want to go as fast as possible and with very little manual work on your part. In today's marketplace, you are constantly flooded with data about your businesses, and AI can help you finally harness, interpret, and act on every touchpoint—if you learn how to use it. The wonder of it all is that you'll be able to create efficiencies by automating repetitive tasks, thus mitigating the risk of human error. You will be able to pivot your team members to other priority tasks as well as more strategic endeavors. There is no doubt that AI can help you make better business decisions. Most importantly, AI enables you to tackle the customer experience head-on to create positive encounters with your products, services, and establishment in a way that was unavailable to small businesses before the technology existed.

As you continue through this book, you'll learn how to easily implement AI into your business through user-friendly and affordable tools. Additionally, you'll see example prompts that will guide you in effectively harnessing these AI tools for practical and innovative business solutions. You'll learn how to mend the dysfunctional parts of your organization, stand out from competitors, and create systems that scale. This is an opportunity to be empowered by new technology to construct a business that aligns with your aspirations.

Chapter 2

Building a Comprehensive AI Strategy

Before you delve into the later chapters on specific applications of artificial intelligence throughout your business, you should take the time to build a comprehensive AI action plan. Implementing AI can involve many evaluation, testing, and implementation steps, but the efforts will be worth it! This book will help you outline all the steps necessary for adopting AI tools for your business. Taking the time to implement a strategy for using this technology will help make your business run better and faster.

ESTABLISH YOUR BUSINESS GOALS

Goals don't always have to be monetary, although these types of goals can certainly help create focus in business. Ask yourself the following questions to determine your business goals:

- If I could fix one thing about my business, what would it be?
- What business problems keep me up at night?
- What do I wish I could do faster in my business?
- What was the most recent major issue in my business, and why did it happen?

- What would a perfectly ordinary day look like for me at work?
- If I had to choose, would I rather increase gross sales or reduce costs?

As you answer these questions, start to note common threads. Disgruntled customers might be a recurring issue affecting your team morale, business reputation, and sales. Or perhaps operational inefficiencies, like human-made errors with data input, keep you up at night and drive up costs. Once you've mulled over your answers, establish three measurable business goals. For example, if disgruntled customers are a common thread, a measurable goal could be to increase customer satisfaction scores by 20% over the next six months through improved customer service training and support processes.

AI in Practice

Let's go through an example scenario with my client Lupe Monroy, a landscape designer based in the Bay Area. She helps suburban families remodel their home exteriors (front and back) and mainly gets her clients via referrals. While the project budgets are sizable, much of the money goes to materials and (third-party) construction teams that Lupe manages. Lupe is paid by the hour to design the concepts and manage a construction team of the client's choosing.

Lupe needs help automating tasks and correspondence in multiple areas of her business, and she can use AI to create systems to take care of these tasks. While a quick email here and there might only be 5 minutes, this can quickly snowball into hours of lost time. For example, if you spend 5 minutes responding to twelve different emails throughout the day, that's already an hour spent solely on emailing.

So, let's summarize Lupe's business goals:

1. Reduce overall working time to increase profit margins by 10%.
2. Increase client conversions by 10% by automating the sales process.
3. Complete construction projects seven days ahead of schedule.

You can see in the upcoming sections how specific AI tools can provide the solutions Lupe needs to improve her business performance.

IDENTIFY WHERE AI CAN ADD VALUE

Now that you've got your business goals, it's time to get creative with potential solutions. In this section, the more ideas you have, the better. Take each goal and brainstorm three or more actions to help you achieve this vision. Don't worry about knowing whether or not AI can actually do the action you're jotting down; we'll get to that part shortly.

Let's revisit the example of Lupe to show you this brainstorming in action. Lupe could benefit from off-loading administrative tasks to reduce her overall working time and increase profit margins by 10%. She can use AI tools to:

- Write her emails.
- Draft her social media content.
- Set up appointments.
- Draft contracts.
- Manage her inbox.

To increase client conversions by 10% by automating her sales process, Lupe can use AI tools to:

- Live chat with potential clients.
- Target prospective clients.
- Suggest keyword improvements on her website.
- Schedule outreach sequences.
- Track conversion rates.
- Follow up with inquiries.
- Do preliminary sales calls. (Yes, you read that right!)

To complete construction projects seven days ahead of schedule, Lupe could utilize project management AI tools to:

- Create onboarding documents for construction teams.
- Design timelines and calendars.

- Track project progress.
- Prioritize tasks.
- Create project schedules.
- Automatically update schedules if there are delays.
- Provide an analysis of working time.
- Establish the next steps from meetings.

As you can see, we now have twenty different potential opportunities to use AI to help Lupe save time and money. And, given the overlap in many of these tasks, we likely won't have to find twenty different tools to help her with this. How do we begin? The first step is to get familiar with generative AI tools.

AI in Action

Use a generative AI tool such as ChatGPT as a thought partner to further your brainstorming. Here is an example of a prompt you can use. I've included Lupe's information, but you can swap in your own answers before submitting them to ChatGPT.

I need help identifying specific opportunities to help me achieve my business goals. Before I specify my request, here is information about me and my business:

I am a landscape designer based in the Bay Area. I help suburban families remodel their home exteriors (front and back), and I mainly get my clients via referrals. While the project budgets are sizable, much of the project budget goes to materials and (third-party) construction teams that I manage. I am paid by the hour to design the concepts and manage a construction team of the client's choosing.

To help you better understand my perspective and goals, here are my answers to the following questions:

- "If I could fix one thing about my business, what would it be?" I'd like to make more money without requiring more time from myself. Since I'm a one-person business not interested in growing my team, my work is capped by my daily hours. I want to find a way to profit more without requiring my clients to increase their budgets.

- "What business problems keep me up at night?" Living in the Bay Area is incredibly expensive. With economic uncertainty constantly mentioned in the news, I worry that landscape design won't be a priority if there's ever a recession. I want to have more of a nest egg in case that happens.

- "What do I wish I could do faster in my business?" The sales and pitching process is essential but takes a long time. I need to develop a relationship with the client to earn trust personally. From a proposal perspective, every client has a unique space, so every pitch I make is done from scratch.

- "What was the most recent major issue in my business, and why did it happen?" I managed a third-party contractor team that my client selected outside my advice. Unfortunately, the contractor team was difficult to manage, requiring much more hands-on direction from me. This ate into my client's budget, and to avoid asking my client for more money, I worked many hours without pay.

- "What would a perfectly ordinary day look like for me at work?" I'd wake up early to work out, and then I'd check my email and see that some leads had filled in a preliminary form and automatically scheduled a call with me. I'd work on some proposals for the rest of the morning before heading out to clients' homes to check in with the contractor teams. I'd work 5–6 hours per day max (including driving time to visit my clients and back) and have a steady income stream.

- "If I had to choose, would I rather increase gross sales or reduce costs?" Ultimately, I'd like to reduce costs by saving my time working.

Based on these answers, I have distilled three core business goals and brainstormed some small tasks AI tools can do to help me achieve these goals.

Please create at least five additional tasks per goal and the new tasks should be ones I haven't mentioned here.

I went through this exercise with ChatGPT. The tool suggested fifteen fantastic ideas for Lupe beyond what was provided, including optimizing travel routes, automating reporting and analysis, expense tracking, automated client profiling, AI-assisted design suggestions, and even integrating weather forecasts into project schedules.

1. Reduce overall working time to increase profit margins by 10%:
   a. Write my emails.
   b. Draft my social media content.
   c. Set up appointments.
   d. Draft contracts.
   e. Manage my inbox.

2. Increase client conversions by 10% by automating the sales process:
   a. Live chat with potential clients.
   b. Target prospective clients.
   c. Suggest keyword improvements on my website.
   d. Schedule outreach sequences.
   e. Track conversion rates.
   f. Follow up with inquiries.
   g. Do preliminary sales calls.

3. Complete construction projects seven days ahead of schedule:
   a. Create onboarding documents for construction teams.
   b. Design timelines and calendars.
   c. Track project progress.
   d. Prioritize tasks.
   e. Create project schedules.
   f. Automatically update schedules if there are delays.
   g. Provide an analysis of working time.
   h. Establish the next steps from meetings.

SELECTING THE BEST AI TOOLS FOR YOUR BUSINESS

Business-specific AI tools belong to a different category than text-based generative AI tools like ChatGPT, Claude, and Gemini. These tools are designed to address particular functions such as marketing, customer service, finance, and inventory management, with new tools frequently emerging to cater to a variety of business needs.

An Overview of Business-Specific AI Tools

Business-specific AI tools often come with interfaces designed for ease of use, even for those with limited technical expertise. Throughout this book, I highlight tools that I consider exceptionally user friendly and powerful based on thorough research and personal experience. While some business-focused AI tools are prompt-based, many are task-specific and intuitive, reducing the learning curve for users. Certain areas, like finance or inventory management, may require more complex setups.

One challenge small business owners face is the trial and experimentation needed to find the right tools for their specific needs. Your time is valuable; most likely you don't have time to test many AI tools. Luckily for you, this book includes handpicked tools that are user friendly and cost effective. However, I also encourage you to explore tools on your own to become comfortable with AI developments. Embracing an experimental mindset and diving into new tools as you hear about them will be an important ongoing process to help you build the best tool kit for your business.

Factors to Consider When Choosing a Tool

Let's first determine your criteria for initially testing AI tools. Here are some of the factors you should consider:

- **Ensure the tool can complete one of your list's intended tasks.** (Ideally, it can do more than one!) You'll see this on the tool's sales page and product reviews. Try doing a quick Google search of "AI for [Insert name of task]" and exploring the results.
- **Identify the user-friendly tools.** At this stage in your AI journey, you want to ease the path of resistance and choose simple tools. This can often be initially determined by what's displayed on the product website. If the copy is straightforward and the visuals are laid out clearly, those are good indicators that it'll be easy to use. Another trick: Peek at the website's footer to see if there's a Help section. If you can see extensive support articles and a live chat support, put the tool on your "to test" list.
- **Watch demos of the product on YouTube.** Creators like me give honest and thorough reviews of AI tools to help business owners like yourself. Use that to your advantage and get a sneak peek of your potential tool in action.

Compatibility with Your Systems

Many popular tools small businesses already use integrate AI, though not always in meaningful ways. Sometimes, these integrations replicate basic functions that could be done with a separate generative AI tool like ChatGPT. If there's a software you currently use that's critical for your business, it's worth seeing if your AI tool is compatible. For example, Monday.com—a comprehensive project management and collaboration platform—is the lifeblood of my agency, and any kind of project management AI tool that gets integrated will need to work with Monday .com. Monday.com organizes tasks, timelines, and team communications, making it essential for coordinating our projects. An AI tool needs to be compatible with Monday.com to efficiently handle outputs such as task updates, timelines, and project statuses. Even if there's not a native integration, I can count on a platform like Zapier, which automates workflows by connecting different apps and services, to link Monday .com with the AI tool in the desired way.

Considering Cost

While the tools in this book are what I believe to be the most cost-effective solutions for small businesses, you should "dot your i's" and "cross your t's" while determining the financial investment that makes the most sense for your organization. AI tools can range widely in cost, from a few hundred to several thousand dollars per year, depending on their complexity and capabilities. When you've found an AI tool that can solve a specific task, it is only then that you move on to consider evaluating the costs and benefits of using the tool. Prices for AI tools change frequently, so it's important to consider the long-term value and return on investment they offer. The efficiency gains and time savings these tools provide can quickly justify the initial investment.

Here's an example: If you currently spend 2 hours per week answering customer inquiries, know that an AI live chat might reduce your customer inquiry time by 50%. If your hourly rate is $100 per hour, a live chat tool that saves you 1 hour every week represents a reduced labor cost of $100 per week, which adds up to $5,200 per year. (Chances are that you'd save more than that, but we'll get into that in Chapter 6.) With these calculations, it is easy to see that any AI tool less than $5,200 per year will likely be a positive ROI, and that doesn't even consider the money you could make once you've freed up 1 hour per week!

You can determine if a tool is a good fit for you by testing it out yourself. That's why I always recommend looking for tools with trial periods of ideally seven days or longer. Just make sure to maximize the free time before committing to an ongoing subscription.

Sharing AI Across Departments

Many functions of business-specific AI tools could be applicable to multiple departments in your business. For example, artificial intelligence's insights can be used to determine what products are created, how customers receive communications, and so much more.

Think of your AI data as a way to unify your entire company, cross-departmentally, with a crystal clear vision of who your customers are and what they want. With artificial intelligence, you can help teams make informed decisions based on customer behavior, and you can even use AI as a way to bust down departmental silos within your company.

For example, the tool Salesforce has the ability to merge insights from a company's customer service and sales departments to ensure that your successful conversions remain happy customers. You can also integrate AI into Slack so your teams get real-time updates about leads who became customers. A great integration for that is Sidekick by Jigso, which also provides ChatGPT access for free. As you think about which AI options might be good for your company, don't forget to think of the overall picture and include as many departments as you can.

CREATE A TIMELINE FOR INTEGRATING AI INTO YOUR BUSINESS

Implementing AI might sound great in theory (and, trust me, it's great in reality!), but adding new tools to your business systems requires a commitment. I find creating a timeline extraordinarily helpful as far as holding yourself accountable for making this change. For a sustainable and meaningful implementation schedule, try a phased approach.

Phase One (Weeks One to Six)

In this phase, you'll want to select one or two tasks from your brainstorming list that you'd like to improve with AI. Begin by researching over one to two weeks. During this time, you'll evaluate your different tool options for each task.

By the end of the two weeks, you should have a list of all the potential AI tools for your task. As you create your list, add notes such as:

- Price (and, ideally, a free trial period).
- Capabilities beyond your immediate task (in case you could use them later).
- Quality of customer service.
- Anything else you've noticed in your research.

Next, take a week to narrow down your options to two to three tools. If you're particularly conscious of costs, I recommend calculating your ROI from improving the task; you can compare this to the tool's fee. (See the Considering Cost section earlier in this chapter.) Feel free to run your short list past partners or trusted colleagues who can take a second look at your selections. If they know you or your business well, hearing their feedback and, especially, any concerns will be helpful.

At this point, you'll be in week four of your AI implementation timeline. Over the next week, carve out some time in your calendar to create accounts for your short list of AI resources. I recommend having one "assignment" to use to test each tool, and then you can compare your experience and the result. This is nearly akin to an interviewing process where you provide a brief assignment to potential candidates. I urge you to wear an exploratory hat when trying out these tools. Follow your curiosity as you feel out the tool. Much of AI is asking yourself, "What happens if?" Do this as much as possible during the trial phase.

As you try out each tool, note what you like and don't like. For example, if you're seeking a tool to help with copywriting, it might be worth compiling each tool's copy result to compare the writing. Run it past colleagues and get their input as well. Ask yourself what went well and what left room to be desired—with the interface and the output.

This is also an excellent opportunity to test the resources and responsiveness of your tool's Help team. If you have a question—any question—seek your answer in articles, email their support team, or use their live chat. Artificial intelligence is fast moving, and you will want a trustworthy support team to help you stay up to speed.

After testing the tools for a week, you'll most likely have a favorite. However, before officially implementing the tool into your business, it could be worth asking a team member to try it for two weeks. Personally, I wouldn't provide any background training to the team members on how to use the tool. Instead, see how the team member can naturally navigate it. In a dream scenario, your tool can be used by almost anyone on your team with relative ease, so a "blind test" can help confirm the best tool for your group's skill set.

By the end of week six, choose your tool (or tools) for your business. Congratulations! Now you're ready to implement.

Phase Two (Weeks Seven to Twelve)

For the first two weeks of officially using your tool(s), do your best to use the tool exclusively. Don't revert to old habits or systems. A crucial part of mastering AI comes from, for lack of a better term, playing with the technology. You'll learn how to use the tool better and faster if you commit to wholly integrating it for your desired task. Your team must do the same thing.

After the two weeks are up and you're feeling more comfortable with the AI tool, you should create clear objectives for what success looks like. As with anything in business, the more you can measure, the more you can learn, so set quantifiable goals related to each tool you adopt.

Here is one of my best ideas: Over the next four weeks, start recording the process of using the AI tool. Create a step-by-step guide, like a standard operating procedure (SOP), focusing on the specific tool. For example, if you use the AI tool for sales outreach, outline the setup process, including drafting messages. Share the instructions with someone unfamiliar with the tool and refine the SOP based on their questions or issues until everything is clear.

Phase Three (Weeks Thirteen Onward)

This phase is all about reviewing and adjusting. You should compare your quantifiable goals to the results of AI. Ask yourself:

- Am I getting the ROI I expected?
- If not, what needs to change?
- What needs to be improved?

- Can this tool do more than we currently have it do?
- Is this still the right tool for me?

From there, continue to tinker with your tools. Many artificial intelligence tools have multiple capabilities, so consider maximizing those features for your business. If you feel like you have your task entirely handled by your new AI tool, then go back to phase one and select one or two more tasks from your list to implement. Rinse and repeat.

Here's the beauty of this phased approach: If followed, you'll have anywhere from four to nine tasks entirely handled by artificial intelligence technology in a year. And with each tool you adopt or feature you implement, you'll find it more accessible and easier to bring AI into your business. If you ever become overwhelmed, remember that every tool should have a customer service team to help you—most likely a chatbot is the first line of response.

DATA, AI, AND YOUR BUSINESS

As you explored in Chapter 1, artificial intelligence requires data to create outputs. That data can come from any source, but for you, that data will obviously come from your business. Here are some examples of data used by common AI technology:

- For any recruitment software (like LinkedIn Talent Insights), the tool will need data about the job posting and each applicant to analyze the candidates for the role.
- To optimize inventory with the help of computer vision technology (like Zoho Inventory), the tool will need data about stock levels and sales.
- To analyze real estate industry and pricing trends (like Zillow), the tool needs to know property and market data to estimate prices.
- To do customer support chats (like Zendesk), the tool will need historical data on customer service interactions.
- To provide healthcare insights and diagnoses (like IBM Watson Health), the tool will need patient medical records and other data points about treatment recommendations.

You can see data's vital role in maximizing AI's capabilities. Without access to market data, Zillow wouldn't be able to do a pricing estimate. Without examples of customer service interactions, Zendesk might provide incorrect or off-brand messages to your customers. In general, AI tools will accept text documents, spreadsheets, and other common formats like CSV, JSON, and Excel. Some tools can also read specialized data formats, such as Epic patient file outputs or Quicken invoices, depending on their specific applications.

You should match the data you have with an AI tool that can process that specific type of data. Also, the cleaner the data, the better AI will be able to perform, so prepare for some potential organization time in advance. A big data cleanup might not sound enticing, but it's worth it. You could also consider employing the work of an artificial intelligence tool to help organize your data. More on that in another chapter.

SCALING YOUR AI SYSTEMS

Most business owners strive to maintain or grow their businesses. If you want to maintain your business, I will assume that you want to reduce costs through money and time. I will also assume that growing your business means that you want to increase your revenues. Either way, it's imperative to consider how you can also scale AI to suit your business.

Performance

If your AI tool is going to be processing a lot of data or tasks, make sure it can handle that volume. "High volume" can vary depending on the context, but generally, it refers to processing large datasets (e.g., millions of records) or performing tasks at a high frequency (e.g., real-time data processing). Consider:

- Confirming performance capabilities with the tool's support team. Tell them the volume you're anticipating and see if they can handle it. For example, if you expect the AI tool to process thousands of customer interactions per day or analyze large datasets with millions of records, inform the support team to ensure their tool can handle such high volumes efficiently.

- Checking in with team members during peak times to ensure optimal performance.
- Requesting a dashboard (again, from the support team) that displays system performance. You might check the dashboard to monitor how quickly the AI tool is processing data or handling tasks, ensuring that it meets your business's needs during high-demand periods.

Ability to Do More Tasks for You

As you consider scaling up, it's usually a good idea to make sure your tool is good at more than one thing. For example, at first glance, Anyword is a copywriting tool. Perhaps you first use this tool to save time on writing copy for your ad campaigns. However, Anyword can also help you:

- Establish your written tone of voice.
- Evaluate your website content.
- Write blog posts.
- Write social media content.
- Write emails, including subject lines.
- Brainstorm SEO-driven YouTube video topics.

So, while Anyword is a fantastic solution for someone who wants to save time with ad campaign copywriting, you can see that this feature is just the tip of the iceberg. You'll be able to easily off-load more and more tasks to Anyword when you're ready, which helps with scaling.

STAY INFORMED

Artificial intelligence is fast moving, and it can feel like there's a new update almost daily. While the tools recommended in this book will undoubtedly help solve your existing business challenges of today, there is a need for all of us to stay educated about the never-ending new developments with AI tools.

To stay in the loop, subscribe to trusted creators (like me!) and AI-focused publications. It's our job to be immersed in the industry and to distill what you need to know. From my social media channels (and particularly YouTube), I create content specifically for small business owners like yourself. I demo the latest tools, provide my honest opinions on what's worth investing in, share industry updates, and more.

Remember to always maintain a sense of experimentation. The beauty of free trials is that, well, they're free. It costs you nothing to make an account and give it a whirl. As an artificial intelligence tool comes on your radar, make a note to take it for a spin. You might like it and you might not, and both scenarios are valuable: You'll either find a new tool for your business, or you'll know the tool isn't right for you.

PART 2

In this next part, you'll find dozens of ideas for how AI can help you tackle critical business functions, complete with stories and exercises to inspire you to take action. These ideas are called *use cases*. First, you'll see AI's potential impact on your customer acquisition pipeline, specifically in sales and marketing. You'll learn how to identify the AI opportunities in your pipeline and see some of the tools and exercises to easily incorporate the technology within your business. You'll learn about artificial intelligence's social media and content creation abilities, such as using AI to write your copy, edit your photos, conduct competitor research, and much more. There will also be an in-depth exploration of AI and customer service, ensuring your current and future customers are cared for as you become more efficient through artificial intelligence.

Next, you'll dive into the many ways you can leverage AI in your business's finances and accounting—including cash flow monitoring, financial forecasting, invoicing, budgeting, and more—with various tool options to suit businesses of all kinds. This book will also review how to improve your business operations and human resources departments through artificial intelligence, from procurement and fulfillment to interviewing candidates. Lastly, you'll uncover AI's benefits for data analysis, security and legal compliance, research and development, and innovation, with plenty of use case examples and step-by-step recommendations for your business to adopt this technology.

Each chapter in Part 2 will give you a complete rundown for how AI can help you overhaul that particular department. I also provide a list of AI platforms that I personally recommend for each task based on my extensive research and testing, along with suggestions of the relevant data or information you might want to have on hand. You'll learn broad and specific ideas, as well as "AI in Practice" examples that showcase how some ideas were implemented by actual businesses. You can implement as many or as few of these use cases as you want. See which ones resonate with you, your staff, your budget, your business, and your time frame and proceed accordingly. Also, you can read each chapter one by one to see what you can glean from it, or you can skip around to chapters dealing with topics you already know are especially relevant to your business. Just like AI, make this book work however it'll be most helpful for you!

Chapter 3

AI + Sales

Even if your business has exemplary sales without artificial intelligence, you are still underperforming compared to what's possible with AI. This chapter will explore how AI can help your small business gather high-quality leads and marketing insights to improve your sales—all while you focus on your products and services. You'll also learn about how AI enables you to build more personal connections with customers, users, and readers. Take advantage of this new technology, and you will most definitely have the tools to get a leg up on the competition!

THE EVOLUTION OF SALES IN THE AI ERA

Without sales, there's no revenue; without revenue, there's no business. These truths may be universally acknowledged; however, traditional sales practices like cold-calling, door-to-door selling, and manual data analysis are no longer the only methods for generating revenue—and frankly, these efforts are not even considered best practices anymore. If you can implement AI solutions effectively, you can say goodbye to manually sifting through customer data and instead make decisions from readily available and deeply analyzed insights. AI is a wonderful tool for automating lead generation and customer segmentation, refining sales funnels, gathering predictive analytics, and personalizing email campaigns for more targeted and efficient outreach to potential customers.

Here are a few good reasons you should (quickly) adopt artificial intelligence technology into your sales practice.

Gain the Competitive Edge

We're at a critical juncture in artificial intelligence; while it's becoming commonplace for businesses to employ AI, it's not universally adopted (yet). So, the sooner you start using AI, the sooner you'll understand the technology and the sooner you'll surpass (and outpace) your competitors. In this way you can stay ahead regarding leads, customer insights, and market trends.

Maximize Human Creativity

Whether you do sales yourself or have a team of twenty, artificial intelligence can help automate mundane or cumbersome tasks to free up time for other efforts. Instead of losing time to note-taking and routine follow-ups, let AI do the heavy lifting so your team can focus on what it does best.

Improve Your Customer Experience

One of the many beautiful things about AI is its ability to create bespoke experiences. Imagine how incredible it would be for a lead (and customer) to be presented with custom-tailored information that speaks to their needs in a voice that aligns with who they are as a client. With artificial intelligence, there are many ways to accomplish this effort; you can use tools to finesse outbound messages based on browsing history, have recommendations generated based on prior purchasing behavior, and even leverage chatbots to provide personalized answers and recommendations based on queries. Some may argue against businesses having access to this level of data, but from my point of view, the capability of delivering exactly what your customer wants is empowering.

Find Data-Rooted Strategies

Artificial intelligence can instantaneously detect trends and deep insights that will supercharge your sales efforts. Your team will be confident in making informed decisions about your sales strategy, and with AI's insights, you'll be able to better understand your customers in a way you could not do without it. There's only so much the human mind can see and decipher with data. Having AI efficiently sort through information provides a small business owner with much more information to leverage on behalf of the client.

AI IN PRACTICE

As business owners (and salespeople), it's easy for us to be unaware of how much manual effort goes into the traditional sales funnel process. Think about email communication and how many messages must be written and responded to in a given week. Before you know it, emails can compound and follow-through can take up so much time. To paint a picture for you of scope creep, let's talk about my client Ashley Haun.

Ashley is a business and lifestyle mentor who helps business owners figure out how to reconfigure their companies to operate successfully without them. Let's walk through what her sales process is like without AI.

Mentorship Sales Process Without AI

- Most of Ashley's leads come from referrals. Outside of referrals, Ashley spends about 1 hour per week researching potential clients and usually finds about four leads.
- When Ashley contacts that referral or potential lead, she sends a manual outreach email. This can take about 15 minutes per message because she wants to get the right tone.
- Ashley currently uses a calendar scheduling tool (like Calendly) so that leads can schedule appointments. (This requires no time from Ashley.)
- Ashley's intro calls with leads take about 30 minutes per person.
- After the intro call, Ashley sends a follow-up email. This takes about 15 minutes to craft.
- After the follow-up email, Ashley spends about 1 hour answering questions, following up, and even doing a second call if necessary.
- If a client wants to move forward, Ashley sends a contract and manually issues an invoice. This takes about 20 minutes per client.
- Ashley uses a notebook to keep track of leads. While she understands where people fall out of her pipeline, she doesn't have concrete numbers to guide decisions.

Without artificial intelligence, every lead takes Ashley about 2 hours to secure from start to finish. If Ashley wants to pursue four leads per week, she will spend over 416 hours per year on sales activity without guaranteed conversions. She clearly needs concrete data to help guide her sales process. Ashley is incredible at closing a deal, but she operates from a place of instinct, which requires mental energy that could be better spent elsewhere.

Mentorship Sales Process with AI

Now, here's what the process could look like if Ashley employs artificial intelligence for every step of her sales process:

- Ashley sets up a referral program on her website through a tool like ReferralCandy, which tracks all potential clients sent by referrers. Any leads who sign up for an intro call on the referral page will get added to Ashley's email list and receive personalized follow-up emails from Salesforce. After the setup, this requires no time from Ashley.
- For lead generation, Ashley first runs data about her existing clients through ChatGPT to analyze common patterns and attributes, which she can then use to guide research. This is a one-time action that takes about 5 minutes total.
- After getting insight from ChatGPT, Ashley uses a combination of LinkedIn Sales Navigator and Salesforce Starter Suite, powered by AI, to manage her lead generation. Within Starter Suite, she can save LinkedIn leads and send outreach messages drafted by a tool like Persado within minutes. The outreach message will have a link to Ashley's Calendly, where they can schedule a time on her calendar.
- For outreach follow-ups, Starter Suite alerts Ashley about leads that need follow-ups, and she can copy and paste a prewritten message from Persado. Each message takes about 2 minutes to send.
- After Ashley has a 30-minute intro call with someone, the lead will automatically get personalized follow-up emails from Starter Suite with a link to purchase services from her website. After purchasing, they'll receive an automatic email to schedule the first coaching call. This requires no time from Ashley.

This is the power of artificial intelligence in action. Ashley can go from spending 2 hours per lead to about 35 minutes, reducing her total time by 70%. Ashley can now use her saved time toward something else. Or, if she wants to continue spending 8 hours per week on sales, she could pursue over seven hundred qualified leads per year. Best of all, the additional leads can potentially convert more often because they're hyper-targeted using AI-informed insights on past clients.

PREFERRED PLATFORMS FOR SALES

Here is a list of some AI tools I recommend to sales departments:

- **Starter Suite.** Salesforce Starter Suite is a simple customer relationship management (CRM) solution offering features like sales forecasting and meeting scheduling. Its AI integrations enhance customer databases by extracting relevant data from email conversations. The "Pay Now" feature allows embedding payment links in emails for quick transactions. Starter Suite also provides ready-to-use sales paths and reports to keep teams on track and manage sales pipelines. This suite helps businesses refine and target leads more effectively, increasing conversion rates.

- **Whatagraph.** Whatagraph is a data visualization and reporting software that simplifies data comprehension and analysis. It transforms raw data into understandable formats like graphs and visuals. Whatagraph also offers predictive analytics, enabling businesses to model future trends based on existing data, aiding in effective planning and decision-making by providing insights into potential future outcomes.

- **ClickFunnels.** The software ClickFunnels is designed to make it easy for businesses to create effective sales funnels that can help increase profits. It enables lead capture at various stages and offers customization options for different types of businesses. Most importantly, small business owners can create their funnel without hiring a developer.

- **Manychat.** Manychat is a chatbot tool that helps content creators improve their sales. It does this by automating lead generation, initiating conversations with the customer, and providing instant customer support. Manychat can help small businesses automate and optimize various aspects of the sales process, leading to increased conversions and revenue.
- **Pipedrive.** Pipedrive uses AI to prioritize deals, recommend actions, and automate repetitive tasks, helping small businesses focus on closing more sales efficiently.
- **Zoho.** Zoho CRM is a comprehensive platform for managing sales pipelines, offering extensive automation features for tracking and follow-up activities. Its AI assistant, Zia, can clean up databases, identify absent leads, complete contact details, automate follow-up emails, send a reminder for in-person appointments, and track post-call actions like sending contracts.

Generate Leads

What AI can do: Review potential leads and create a list of those who are most likely to become customers.

Recommended AI tools for this task: ChatGPT, ZoomInfo, Clearbit, HubSpot's Sales Hub

Data you might need on hand: Customer interactions, sales history, marketing efforts (e.g., customer contact information, purchase history, website analytics, social media engagement metrics, and details of past marketing campaigns)

Lead generation is one key area of sales where AI can make a big impact. Instead of trawling through databases manually, the algorithms of AI software can find potential customers on your behalf. Predictive analytics use customer data to forecast who will most likely make a purchase within a given timeline. As a small business owner, you can use the convenience of AI to then focus your energy where impact is high—on leads with the highest potential of converting. Automated lead generation and actionable customer insights were once wishful thinking, but now they're a tangible reality.

Define Your Ideal Customer

Regardless of industry, lead generation is typically the starting point of any sales process. Previously for your business, this may have involved cold calls, trade shows, door-to-door sales, or social media ads using manual lead tracking (like a good ol' spreadsheet).

With AI, this process can be completely optimized and automated. Algorithms can now scour the Internet and niche databases almost instantly to find qualified leads using preset criteria, like industry, location, needs, budget, or other characteristics to help you pinpoint your ideal customer.

Try asking a generative AI platform, such as ChatGPT, what key criteria are worth considering for your target audience. Better yet, provide details on your business goals, product or service information, existing customer demographics, geographical focus, and budget, and it should provide a more detailed answer. You can even share a few stories or specific customers or clients. Then, let AI work its magic through a summary of your ideal clientele in mere minutes.

AI in Action

Try this prompt to pinpoint your ideal customer:

 I need you to identify and summarize important criteria for my target audience, including demographic information such as location, industry, and budget. Please ask me brief questions so I can get you information to provide a comprehensive overview.

An open-ended prompt like this will outline what information you should provide the chat so it can describe important criteria for you to consider when identifying and gathering leads. It's helpful to provide AI

examples of the type of criteria you're looking for (like location, industry, and budget) so it understands the data value you seek. Beyond that, by prompting AI to ask you brief questions, it ensures that no "assumptions" are made on AI's part, which will help you get the information you need with minimal back-and-forth.

 Now that you know more about my target audience, please summarize:

- **The three things they'd like most about what my company offers.**
- **The three hesitations they'd have about my company.**
- **The three things that keep them up at night.**

Generative AI can help you craft a compelling message that speaks directly to your ideal customer. By anticipating what's most important to them, you'll be better able to demonstrate how you're the best solution for the lead's needs.

Once you've identified the ideal criteria to consider, you can use a specialized AI platform, such as ZoomInfo or Clearbit, to gather leads. When the leads are identified, an AI-enhanced CRM software like HubSpot's Sales Hub is handy for managing contact information.

Sell More Effectively to Existing Customers

An oft-forgotten part of sales is selling to existing clientele. AI can assist with this effort by keeping tabs on satisfied and disgruntled customers. AI's technology can unpack key insights from interactions with customers and glean even more helpful information to boost your sales search. This element of AI technology is called natural language processing (NLP), which you learned about in Chapter 1, and with the right direction, it can analyze interactions with customers who are already engaging with your business by way of email, social media comments, and even reviews.

The possible outcomes from using NLP can be overwhelming, so let's go through a quick scenario: Imagine you run an e-commerce jewelry company with an active social media presence. You employ an NLP-powered social media monitoring tool to continuously track mentions of your company and related keywords, such as *necklace, bracelet*, and *ring*. The NLP tool identifies mentions and performs sentiment analysis on these mentions—categorizing them into positive, negative, or neutral sentiments. For instance, a post that reads, "I love the new line of necklaces from [Your Company Name]!" would be categorized as positive sentiment, and that user can be flagged as a lead for future launches. On the other hand, while not always fun, sifting through AI-collected negative statements about your brand can present opportunities to repair relationships with a previously loyal customer.

Predict Customer Behavior

What AI can do: Analyze past consumer behavior and social media activity to predict future outcomes.

Recommended AI tools for this task: Whatagraph

Data you might need on hand: Historical sales data

While it's not possible to read your customers' minds, predictive analytics are arguably the next best thing. These tools can use past behaviors and social media activity to predict future outcomes, informing your sales team's priorities and efforts. AI's predictive analytics blends a few reliable statistical methods to help forecast what will or won't succeed in each demographic. Suppose a segment of customers frequently interacts with posts about eco-friendly products. Predictive analytics can project a higher likelihood of these customers responding positively to a new line of sustainable goods.

Predictive analytics also helps with customer segmentation, lead scoring, and even churn prediction. Instead of your business executing a product launch that isn't working, AI can help you adjust in the early or even middle stages of your campaign to improve target accuracy and help companies like yours make better decisions.

For example, a coffee shop owner might want to introduce a new latte flavor. Based on prior flavor launches, they know that 60% of new flavors succeed. They've even found that providing free samples of a new flavor increases the chance of success by 85%.

Here's where AI comes in: By using predictive analytics within AI, the coffee shop owner could employ machine-learning algorithms to analyze both the historical data of previous flavor launches *and* the new evidence regarding free samples. The model could factor in variables such as customer demographics, seasonal trends, and social media engagement to predict the probable success rate of the new latte flavor. Furthermore, some models could update these predictions in real time as more data becomes available, such as customer feedback on the free samples. In this way, predictive analytics allows the coffee shop owner to make more informed decisions and course corrections if necessary, optimizing the likelihood of the new flavor's success in the market.

Optimize Your Sales Funnel

What AI can do: Research and analyze specific data points along the customer journey to identify where you can make improvements.

Recommended AI tools for this task: ClickFunnels, ZoomInfo

Data you might need on hand: Customer information

A sales funnel is a common way of visualizing the customer journey, starting from awareness all the way through to making the sale—working down each level to the purchase. AI can be used to research and analyze data points along the customer journey to reveal choke points where potential customers drop out of the process. The exact point of customer drop-off has always been challenging to determine for marketers. Nowadays, an AI tool can analyze user behavior on an e-commerce site and suggest when to offer a discount or a free trial, thereby reducing attrition and instead increasing conversions.

In the past, marketers may have relied on basic key performance indicators (KPIs) to gauge customer behavior, including page views, time spent on a page, bounce rate, and shopping cart abandonment rate (calculated by dividing the number of completed purchases by the number of shopping carts created). These metrics provide surface-level insight, and while great on paper, this data falls short of identifying what causes the behavior behind these metrics.

Today, artificial intelligence gives us the tools to optimize, quite literally, every step of the sales funnel. Whether you're getting insights that perhaps your human mind missed or you're getting live email optimizations, artificial intelligence can be the conductor orchestrating your sales symphony.

Sales funnels can be complex, so the following sections will highlight the key advantages of integrating artificial intelligence into your customer's journey.

Score Your Leads

Lead scoring essentially "scores" your leads based on their potential to convert. Multiple indicators, mainly behavioral, are used to arrive at this metric, including their engagement levels on your website, product pages, and emails. This system helps your sales teams know who to prioritize as leads. Having an AI-created lead score means they no longer have to guess at people's intents, budgets, and likelihood to convert.

Better Understand Your Customers

When you use artificial intelligence in your sales funnel, you receive unparalleled insight into your potential and current customers. Aside from collecting data about the behavior on your website, artificial intelligence can also predict *when* a customer will make their next purchase based on past purchase data. Think of the possibilities! Not only will you know when a customer will likely purchase a product; you can also anticipate some extra add-on items that might pique their interest.

Increase Your Conversion Rates

Think of each step in your sales funnel as an opportunity to convert leads to the next stage. Let's say your sales funnel has four parts:

1. **General awareness,** where the lead sees a social media post.
2. **Interest,** where they spend time browsing your site.
3. **Deliberation,** where they add a product to their cart.
4. **Action,** where they purchase the product.

Whether you're aware of it or not, each one of those stages has its own conversion rate. For this example, let's explore what happens if you have a 1% conversion rate at every stage. To convert one customer, you would need:

1,000,000 people seeing your social media post
10,000 people visiting your website
100 people adding an item to their cart
= 1 customer

The odds of you having a 1% conversion rate at every stage of your funnel are slim. It will vary. But, by taking the time to understand every stage of your funnel, you will get a realistic understanding of the actual number of leads that need to be generated to capture a customer.

Let's say you encounter many people adding your products to their cart, but few are completing the purchase. This scenario may indicate that your pricing is too high. AI tools and technology can help you determine what price makes people complete their checkout, and these tools can also calculate your conversion rates at each stage of the funnel, empowering you to choose which funnel part you want to fix first. Look what happens if you were to double the conversion rate to 2% at one stage by improving your website and making your products look more enticing (with the help of AI):

1,000,000 people seeing your social media post
10,000 people visiting your improved website
200 people adding an item to their cart
= 2 customers

That fix at one stage in your funnel doubled your sales. Imagine the possibilities if AI provided real-time observations on your sales funnel's stages and you employed tools to improve each stage based on insights about your customers' behaviors. Your sales process would never be the same.

Better Utilize Your Team

As this book has mentioned, artificial intelligence is unmatched when it comes to efficiency. AI will free up your sales team from day-to-day drudgery and reduce the mental load associated with strategic and creative sales efforts. Instead of facing countless rejections with unqualified leads, your sales reps will be speaking with leads that are pre-vetted for your offering, thereby ensuring the greater possibility of successful conversion.

Better Adapt to Change

Whether your business is seasonal, going through a rough patch, or facing a new competitor coming onto the market, artificial intelligence is a second brain that can immediately adapt to change. For example, if a new trend arises that's relevant to your product or service, AI can notify you about a content marketing opportunity. This could be achieved by scanning social media mentions (with a tool like Brand24) and detecting a surge in discussions about a particular topic related to your industry. It can also detect a change in behavioral patterns, which might prompt you to push new content through email marketing and your website. AI can also, importantly, notice changes in purchasing behavior. These dynamic adaptations in your sales funnel will put you light-years ahead of your competitors—and your previous sales benchmarks as a business.

Use Chatbots for Sales Support

What AI can do: Answer routine customer questions.

Recommended AI tools for this task: Manychat, Zendesk, Intercom

Data you might need on hand: Customer information (such as user profiles and interaction history), knowledge base (such as product/service information and support documentation), company processes (such as business workflows and integration details)

Imagine a dedicated sales associate who works 24/7, answering queries and helping to close sales. Without exaggeration, that's what an AI-powered chatbot can do! Chatbots handle routine inquiries, freeing up your sales team to focus on more relational tasks that are better performed by humans. Chatbots are more than a digital secretary. They can help boost the bottom line of small businesses and even personal brands.

For instance, take my client Juli Bauer Roth, a lifestyle creator behind the brand PaleOMG. She introduced the popular chatbot Manychat into her workflow to automatically send a message to any follower that comments or messages a trigger word (like "App") on an Instagram feed post (which Juli encourages in her caption). The bot replies with an automated comment letting them know they'll get a direct message with information about her product. Then it sends the sign-up information to their direct message inbox. This workflow is a simple yet powerful example of automation that curbs the need for manual engagement.

Forecast Sales

What AI can do: Combine historical data, consumer behavior, market trends, and social media sentiment to make real-time sales forecasts.

Recommended AI tools for this task: Salesforce Starter Suite, Brand24

Data you might need on hand: Historical sales data, customer interaction history, social media sentiment data, market trends and analytics

Don't you wish you could wave a magic wand and know what your future sales would look like? Well, with artificial intelligence, it's somewhat possible.

Traditional forecasting models rely solely on historical data to anticipate future sales. While the general reference is helpful, it's only a fraction of the data points that are necessary for truly accurate predictions. Artificial intelligence merges historical data, consumer behavior, market trends, and social media sentiment to make forecasts that are updated in real time. If you know you will be introducing a new product, you can time that product's release with the forecasts that artificial intelligence provides. You can also make key business decisions, like expanding your team, based on forecasted sales data.

Track Sales

What AI can do: Obtain detailed data about sales tracking.

Recommended AI tools for this task: Salesforce Starter Suite, Zoho CRM, HubSpot, Pipedrive

Data you might need on hand: Sales transaction data, customer interaction logs, conversion rates, sales funnel data

To scale your AI operations over time, you'll want to ensure you have a finger on the pulse of artificial intelligence's insights about your company. These are the main data points you should keep an eye on. Consider tracking your rates pre- and post-AI implementation, and then continue to check in on these data points regularly once your business is using artificial intelligence for sales.

- **Lead conversion rate:** At a high level, you'll want to understand what percentage of leads become customers. At a micro level, you'll want to understand the conversion rate at each step of your pipeline.
- **Sales cycle time:** Determine how long it takes to convert a sale from the moment there's an inquiry until the payment is made. With artificial intelligence in your back pocket, this number should decrease after implementation.

- **Closes per salesperson:** Again, AI isn't taking anyone's job away. In fact, artificial intelligence should help your salespeople close even more sales in a period. If someone's sales are dropping, that's an indicator that they might need help adjusting to the system or you need to find a different AI tool.
- **Closes per department:** AI should help unify teams by providing crystal clear insights on your sales funnel, leads, and existing customers. If sales aren't increasing, that might be a sign that your team isn't maximizing your artificial intelligence tool's data about your business.
- **Sales per product or service:** Monitor the total sales for each product or service you offer. Take note of any offerings that do especially well after implementing artificial intelligence and then apply those insights to your other suite of offerings.

Artificial intelligence is redefining the landscape of sales. With AI on your team, there's no more guessing, hunches, arduous emails, time-taxing follow-ups, or manual tracking. Instead of trying to make sense of thousands of data points, artificial intelligence hands you everything you need to know on a silver platter.

Chapter 4

AI + Marketing and Advertising

The days of relying solely on billboards, radio ads, and direct mailers as the primary marketing strategies are over. AI is revolutionizing marketing by using data to personalize ads, predict trends, and meet consumer needs. Unlike making billboards without any real data—which feels like shouting into emptiness—using AI speaks directly to those interested. It almost reads the minds of potential customers and anticipates their needs.

It's no secret that marketing is competitive. With just one effective campaign by your competitor, all your potential leads could be swept away. That's why leveraging artificial intelligence for your marketing and advertising efforts is vital. You'll stay ahead of the competition and operate from a place of pure precision. This chapter will explore the tools for crafting effective AI-driven marketing strategies.

THE NEW AGE OF MARKETING

Fusing artificial intelligence into your marketing strategy can almost make you feel like you're a mind reader. For example, imagine you own a hardware store. Every customer who comes into your location has different needs. One might be looking for a hammer. Another might just be browsing. A few might want ideas for an upcoming bathroom renovation. Some might be intrigued by smaller supplies near your cashier. In the old days of marketing, you would need to note each customer's preferences manually. There would be immense pressure on you to remember not only each customer but also exactly why they were in your store in the first place.

AI in marketing operates similarly, but it ultimately shoulders the mental load of anticipating, observing, and remembering your customers' preferences. For example, artificial intelligence can note what the customers look at on your website (such as a particular category or product), determine if customers have a specific preference (such as a color or style), and then create precise customer segments based on those behaviors and choices. Even better: Artificial intelligence will automatically update those segments over time as more data is collected, ensuring you always have a firm understanding of your potential customers.

PREFERRED PLATFORMS FOR MARKETING

Here is a list of some AI tools I recommend to marketing departments:

- **Adobe Express.** Adobe Express is my preferred design and content creation tool for small businesses. Its ease of use allows you to quickly create and customize your brand assets using sophisticated templates tailored to your preferences. With AI-powered design tools, it automates tasks like resizing and layout adjustments, making the workflow more efficient. Additionally, its brand management features let you save and apply your brand's colors, fonts, and logos across all materials, ensuring a consistent visual identity throughout your marketing campaigns.
- **Flodesk.** Flodesk is an email marketing platform designed to help small businesses create beautiful, engaging emails with ease. It stands out for its user-friendly interface and stunning templates, allowing businesses to design visually appealing emails without any technical expertise. Flodesk's automation workflows enable small businesses to nurture leads and customers at different stages, helping improve engagement and conversions. Additionally, its flat-rate pricing and unlimited email sending make it an affordable option

for businesses of all sizes. With customizable forms and built-in analytics, Flodesk makes it easy to grow and track email lists while maintaining consistent branding.

- **Klaviyo.** Klaviyo is a marketing automation platform that helps e-commerce brands facilitate email and SMS marketing. It offers customer segmentation as a standout feature, which allows small businesses to sort customers based on demographics (age, gender, or location), behavior (purchase history or browsing patterns), or psychographics (interests, values, or beliefs). This customer segmentation hallmark makes it easy to send personalized marketing messages, leading to a higher ROI in email campaigns.

- **AdQuick.** AdQuick is an out-of-home advertising platform that makes it easy to buy billboard spots worldwide. Their AdQuick AI assistant leverages local information (like behavioral data) to pinpoint audience groups that will respond well to your business advertising.

Implement AI-Driven Marketing Strategies

What AI can do: Track marketing programs, segment your customers, and personalize your marketing to better reach customers.

Recommended AI tools for this task: Flodesk, Klaviyo, Mailchimp, HubSpot

Data you might need on hand: Customer demographics, customer purchasing history, other channel-specific data

Artificial intelligence can enhance all the best parts of a robust marketing strategy. Let's dive into the parts.

Customized Content

Natural language processing features in AI often play a critical role in marketing. You can tailor your content creation through AI based on your audience's real-time preferences and behaviors. If there's a relevant market trend in your industry, artificial intelligence is savvy enough to alter your content messaging to incorporate that trend and present it in a way that is relevant to a specific segment.

Enhanced Customer Segmentation and Behavior Predictions

Artificial intelligence is so tuned into your potential customers that it can distill factors like demographic data, interests, online behavior, and more to inform your content marketing strategy. For example, instead of guessing what tone of voice will resonate most with your audience, artificial intelligence figures that out for you. Instead of depending on the usual A/B testing method, where you compare different versions (A and B) to see which one works better, artificial intelligence can suggest improvements for each specific group of people it identifies in a highly targeted way. For example, popular marketing platforms like Mailchimp use AI to analyze user behavior and deliver personalized content and experiences to different segments of your audience.

Additionally, AI uses data-driven insights to forecast consumer behavior, especially when your marketing team is promoting a specific product or service. It assesses the likelihood of a segment making a purchase. Consider the impact on your next marketing campaign: You'll know the probability of a customer buying your products and receive AI-guided advice on the most effective content to attract that specific customer.

Brand Identity Creation

No AI tool can fully replace the expertise of a skilled designer in crafting your brand identity. I believe the optimal solution is to combine the talents of a proficient designer with artificial intelligence for any branding project. For example, AI can analyze market trends and consumer preferences to provide data-driven insights that guide the designer's creative process. Working together, the combination of human touch and technology can create a very successful design that will make a strong first impression.

Conceptualization and Design for Marketing Campaigns

Artificial intelligence's genius lies in creating efficiencies for your campaigns; it is not a replacement for human direction. You can use AI to generate your copy and images, but it's critical that you direct, guide, and review artificial intelligence's creation to capture your brand's personality.

Email Campaigns

Email marketing campaigns are a fundamental asset in any brand's marketing strategy. Directly reaching customers via email is preferable to relying on "rented land," like social media platforms controlled by big tech companies. Most small business owners don't know that email marketing campaigns can be majorly enhanced with AI features that include determining the best time to send emails, predicting open rates, and suggesting personalized content, to name a few.

AI in Action

Try this series of prompts:

 Prompt 1: Analyze the tone of voice and writing style of the following text: [Paste text that represents your tone of voice and writing style, such as a blog post, social media caption, or email].

 Prompt 2: Use the tone of voice and writing style you've identified to write an email that [Describe your goals for the email].

AI can help you self-identify your writing style and tone of voice, increasing the likelihood that it can generate content that sounds like you or your brand.

Content Personalization

One-size-fits-all advertisements and marketing emails are becoming passé. With AI, content personalization can leverage customer segments to send tailor-made content to groups or individuals. This tool is more than merely adding a customer's name to an email list; it is next level—crafting messages that speak to the user's unique needs and preferences.

My friend Matt Ruggieri founded Onekind, a popular skincare and beauty brand. Matt relies on personalized content to grab his potential buyer's attention. On the brand's website, users can complete a quiz that prescribes a "skin ritual" based on their unique needs. The user receives a discount coupon for completing the quiz, and the brand's marketing team is now equipped with behavioral information that can fuel personalized, unique content for future email and marketing communication.

AI in Action

Try this prompt:

> **Come up with two compelling subject lines I can A/B test based on the following email: [Insert or describe email].**

A/B testing your subject lines is an easy way to boost your open rates by using data to determine the kind of content that resonates most with your audience. This prompt will help you create two different options to try.

Boost Traditional Marketing Methods

What AI can do: Predict what campaigns will be most effective based on your company's marketing history and its knowledge of your marketplace.

Recommended AI tools for this task: Persado

Data you might need on hand: Customer demographics, customer purchasing data, historical data on performance, market trends and analytics

While it may seem counterintuitive, you can apply AI's capabilities to traditional marketing methods, including print and outdoor advertising. Traditional marketing methods, while familiar, are somewhat risky. For example, unlike digital marketing, you can't adjust copy on the fly if a print advertisement isn't performing. Most of the time, you have to run on the instinct of what you *think* will do well. In previous chapters, you've seen how artificial intelligence can make performance predictions based on data. Those predictions can also be used to fuel decisions with traditional marketing, ultimately helping you avoid costly mistakes while also maximizing impact.

Enhanced Precision

The "gamble" you've previously felt with traditional marketing methods can become more of a calculated risk with artificial intelligence. Creating billboards without proper data really is like shouting into emptiness, as I mentioned at the beginning of this chapter. But using AI to inform your billboard strategy is a smart way to ensure your message reaches the right audience. Consider how AI's data processing capabilities could help synthesize traffic and demographic patterns for a billboard advertisement. Instead of going off a hunch of what copy would work best for your billboard, AI could synthesize demographic information with absolute precision to help you understand detailed demographics of who would see the billboard, including age, interests, and even income levels. From there, AI technology could recommend campaign angles that most effectively speak to your target audience. Beyond that, AI could analyze the data from past campaigns to help shape your current and future campaign strategies.

Improved Personalization

With digital marketing, the ability to personalize ads is as simple as an A/B test. Imagine leveraging artificial intelligence's insights to extend personalization into your traditional marketing efforts. Using, again, artificial intelligence's unparalleled abilities to interpret and synthesize immense amounts of data, it's now easier than ever to create print ads that speak to your ideal customer. Let's say you run a clothing boutique. You could use AI to analyze past purchases and segment your customers. Each segment could receive a mail-home product catalog with items that AI recommends for that particular segment, increasing the odds that they'll be intrigued enough to purchase from your store again.

Multiple AI tools can help you with this type of segmentation and marketing. If you integrate your in-person and online purchases with tools like Mailchimp or Klaviyo, their AI-powered algorithms can segment your customers based on preferences, buying patterns, and more. After artificial intelligence has identified your segments, you can create product recommendations that can be used for a print catalog.

Data-Informed Decision-Making

AI's traditional marketing support isn't limited to print ads; it can help inform your decisions with radio advertising too. If you own a car dealership that does radio ad campaigns, artificial intelligence can provide additional insights into the effectiveness of the ads. Instead of hoping for the best after your radio ad runs, artificial intelligence can monitor call volume, website traffic, and in-person visits to measure the effectiveness of the ad. Better yet, artificial intelligence can help you measure the effectiveness of multiple radio ads so you understand what promotions and styles lead to the most results.

Multiple tools can be used concurrently in this example. CallRail is an artificial intelligence tool that can analyze calls, detect call volume changes after an ad, and even track keywords within calls to understand intent better. Placer.ai monitors in-person traffic and can pinpoint any visitor changes after airing an ad.

Supercharge Your Telemarketing

What AI can do: Help decide who you should call, when, and what you should say.

Recommended AI tools for this task: LeadFuze, ZoomInfo, Freshsales, Google Analytics + ChatGPT, Clearbit, Zoho CRM, Boomerang, Seismic, Mindtickle, Auto Dialer from VoiceSpin

Data you might need on hand: Customer purchasing history, customer interaction logs, call scripts, customer demographics

In a world filled with emails, texts, and social media DMs, phone call communications can be a beautifully human way of standing out. Whether you want to connect with new clients, touch base with former ones, or even remind people about appointments, artificial intelligence can complement your telemarketing efforts to make every second count. And if you aren't using telemarketing in your promotional efforts, my hope is that this section will open your eyes to a potential new business generation channel—bolstered through the power of AI.

The Who/What/Where/Why/When/Hows of Telemarketing

Telemarketing might seem like a simple phone call, but multiple complexities need to be considered with a campaign, and—you guessed it—AI can amplify those efforts. This section will give a quick overview of the crucial facets of any telemarketing effort. Then you'll see how artificial intelligence can save you time, guesswork, and, potentially, lost revenues through its technology.

In any telemarketing effort, business owners must consider:

- **Who do you want to target?** Before starting any telemarketing effort, you must consider who you're trying to reach. Are you opening a new store location and want to drum up local business? Do you have a new product and want to connect with former customers? The more specific your customer segment, the better (and, yes, AI can help you figure that out).
- **Why are you calling?** This will be closely intertwined with your answer to the first question. Your call must have a goal outcome, such as preventing no-shows (reminding people of their appointments) or conducting a survey. Your purpose will impact your script, which will impact your results.
- **When should you call?** The time you call can potentially make or break your telemarketing campaign. If you make a daytime call when a busy professional is at the office, you'll be lost among other voicemails. Call in the morning, and you might catch a stressed parent whose kids are late for school. Artificial intelligence can

help you understand and measure the best times to call your ideal customer segments, improve your chances of connecting with them, and, importantly, catch them in a good mood.

- **What will you say?** We've all experienced an aggressive telemarketing call, and it's not pleasant. You'll need a natural script aligned with your business goals to ensure you positively impact your present or potential customers.

- **What happens when you achieve your goal?** If the call goes as you hope, it's vital to have systems to move the customer further down your funnel. This might involve scheduling a follow-up call, booking an appointment or visit, or sending a contract. Artificial intelligence can help you automate these pieces so you can benefit from the momentum of an excited customer.

- **How will you measure success?** A telemarketing campaign can be time intensive. You'll want to be able to quickly determine what success looks like while also developing the infrastructure to track data along the way. It probably comes as no surprise here, but artificial intelligence's genius especially shines here.

- **How will you train your team?** As with most business functions, you'll want to figure out how to scale your telemarketing efforts. AI technology can help you with training and measure the quality of team members' calls to help everyone improve.

- **How will you comply with privacy laws?** Many countries have strict laws about telemarketing, and knowing what you can and cannot do before a telemarketing campaign is essential. Artificial intelligence can bring you up to speed if you don't have a lawyer in-house.

AI in Action

Try this prompt:

 I am a local small business specializing in selling speakers and audio equipment. After analyzing my Google Analytics data, I've found that my most-sold items in 2022 were small home wireless speakers under $500, and my most-viewed pages are for home surround sound speakers. For my upcoming telemarketing campaign, I need creative promotion ideas or items to discount. These should align with the preferences indicated by my sales trends. Do you have any suggestions for promotions that could entice my former customers to repurchase?

AI Tools for Telemarketing

Artificial intelligence helps you understand your customers' needs in a detailed and objective way. Through data, you'll be able to exercise more empathy with your customers than ever before. Let's explore how artificial intelligence tools can help you with each of the previous telemarketing facets. One thing to consider: Even if you aren't using (or don't plan to use) telemarketing for your business, these tools can parlay into other marketing functions. So don't skip ahead!

- **LeadFuze.** This is a customer database tool powered by artificial intelligence. You can run complex searches, including phone numbers, to find your ideal customers. A tool like this would be great for finding people to cold-call because it identifies potential customers who are more likely to be interested in your products or services.
- **ZoomInfo.** If you're in the B2B space, you might want to check out ZoomInfo, an AI-powered database tool that can help you find contact information of people in key company roles and/or industries. In 2019, the platform combined with DiscoverOrg, which offers detailed organizational charts for corporations and

now direct dials with ZoomInfo's extensive company and contact information. The integrated platform offers a more comprehensive solution for B2B sales and marketing professionals seeking accurate and in-depth data for lead generation and market research.

- **Freshsales.** If you want to re-engage old clients, you might want to consider Freshsales. You'll import previous customer data and then Freshsales's AI technology will apply a "score" to each client based on their likelihood of repurchasing from your business. This method enables businesses to prioritize and focus their efforts on high-intent leads or clients most likely to re-engage.

- **Google Analytics + ChatGPT.** For ideas of what to sell in your telemarketing campaign, consider combining Google Analytics and ChatGPT. Google Analytics uses AI to analyze visitor behaviors and sales trends, giving you a deeper understanding of what people like and what people are buying. Then, you can run those results through ChatGPT. Use your Google Analytics insights to tailor this prompt to your specific needs.

- **Clearbit.** Clearbit's technology capitalizes on AI's data accumulation and analysis. It efficiently captures and analyzes your sales interactions and emails, pinpointing the most effective times to engage with your prospects. Beyond this, Clearbit offers actionable suggestions to refine your communication strategies and accurately forecasts the likelihood of success in your sales endeavors.

- **Boomerang.** Boomerang is a comprehensive sales pipeline platform with extensive automation features like tracking and follow-up based on customer job movements. It also includes AI-powered capabilities for tasks such as cleaning databases, identifying absent leads, and filling in gaps for incomplete contact details.

- **Seismic.** This technology functions as an effective trainer and coach for new team members. With Seismic, you can design tailored training modules, incorporating diverse elements like quizzes and various call scenarios. It also enables you to assign diverse lessons, including role-play, written materials, and real-life situations. Beyond these training tools, Seismic effectively tracks and analyzes team performance, providing detailed insights into where each individual shines and areas where they might need more support.

- **Mindtickle.** Mindtickle is a one-stop shop for sales tracking and training. Its AI technology focuses on sales readiness, complete with training, coaching, tracking, call insights, and forecasting. The platform includes a variety of training modules, such as quizzes and scenario-based exercises, and allows for the assignment of diverse lessons including role-plays and real-life situations.

- **Auto Dialer from VoiceSpin.** This platform helps you automate your entire call process and can filter for Do Not Call lists— ensuring maximum legal compliance. The tool uses speech analytics to improve your communication, resulting in a better understanding of customer needs and boosted sales.

Try ChatGPT for Script Creation

While I encourage you to try out all of the tools just discussed to automate and augment your telemarketing business efforts, please remember that ChatGPT (like its competitors) may be the more accessible (and valuable) resource and thought partner. Don't shy away from using ChatGPT to brainstorm approaches to your call scripts. Try out different angles and, with help from one of the previous tools, get feedback on how to finesse your future scripts to increase the likelihood of conversions.

AI in Action

Try a variation of this prompt:

 I'm running a small business focusing on eco-friendly products. I need some innovative ideas for a telemarketing script that highlights our commitment to sustainability, while also being engaging and persuasive.

Make the Most of Trade Shows

What AI can do: Brainstorm aesthetics, sales tactics, and follow-up plans.

Recommended AI tools for this task: ChatGPT, Adobe Express, Adobe Firefly, Salesforce, HubSpot

Data you might need on hand: Product information, marketing materials, trade show objectives, follow-up procedures

Trade shows can be an excellent opportunity for small businesses—but great opportunities can also bring significant risk. A trade show can be a juggling act for even the most competent business owner, where you have multiple goals to maximize the day, weekend, or week.

For instance, if you have a booth at a trade show, there are multiple considerations you'll need to manage. First, from an aesthetics standpoint, your booth must stand out in a likely packed hall—complete with your competitors—and you'll need to have all signs, objects, and technology in hand before you even step into the building. You'll also want to ensure that your team converts ideal customers while also networking with industry colleagues and balancing multiple sales pipelines with different customer segments. Your brand, products, and service messaging and presentation must be perfect, ensuring the right message connects with your target audience. As a brand strategist, addressing these challenges is a frequent and essential part of my work with clients.

Beyond the logistics of setting up the trade show, wowing everyone who walks by your booth, and meaningfully connecting with prospective partners and customers, you'll then need to figure out a prompt follow-up strategy to solidify your connection or sale. All of this in a concentrated time period. It's a lot of pressure, to say the least.

Brainstorming for Trade Show Success

It's easy to think that the onus of brainstorming needs to fall on you, the business owner. Throughout this book, I will continue to remind you of generative AI's usefulness as a brainstorming partner. Think of tools like ChatGPT as a colleague on Microsoft Teams or Slack and be amazed by the thoughtful discussion.

Here is a real discussion a client of mine, Katy, had with ChatGPT to discuss the next Prego Expo.

AI in Action

The prompt she tried:

 I am the founder of Undefining Motherhood. We're an editorial company that empowers moms to care for themselves through accessible, supportive, judgment-free information. We like to say we're powered by both research and heart.

My business is comprised of multiple verticals:

- **Website:** Our articles range from categories like trying to conceive, infertility, birth, miscarriage, stillbirth, infant loss, pregnancy, postpartum, parenting, women's health, lifestyle, book recommendations, and gift guides. The business has a writing team and we generate revenue through ads, affiliate commissions, and sponsored content.

- **Social media:** I post on Instagram and TikTok, and I have a newsletter. We have an avid community and I do sponsored content deals with the right partners.

- ***Expecting & Organized* pregnancy planner:** I sell a pregnancy planner (in digital and print forms) that is very successful.

I am going to have a booth at the upcoming Prego Expo trade show and I need some ideas to make us stand out. My end goal is to promote my planner as much as possible to industry experts and to potential customers to generate exposure.

Can you please come up with ideas? I have a limited budget for the event but will invest when it makes sense for my business.

The response she received:

Creating a memorable and effective presence at the upcoming Prego Expo for Undefining Motherhood, especially with a focus on promoting the *Expecting & Organized* pregnancy planner, can be achieved through several strategic and creative approaches:

Interactive Booth Design:

- **Theme:** Design the booth with a cozy, welcoming theme that resonates with motherhood. Think soft colors, comfortable seating, and warm lighting.

- **Digital Displays:** Use screens to showcase testimonials, planner previews, and snippets from your most impactful articles.

- **Interactive Elements:** Include a touch screen where visitors can navigate through a digital version of your planner or website.

Engaging Activities:

- **Live Q&A Sessions:** Host mini-sessions where you or your team members talk about key topics from your website and answer questions.

- **Planner Customization Station:** Allow visitors to experience a mock-up of customizing the planner. This could be a digital setup or a physical one with stickers, markers, etc.

Promotional Materials:

- **Branded Giveaways:** Offer small, branded items like pens, notepads, or stickers. These are cost effective and can be widely distributed.
- **Discount Vouchers:** Hand out discount codes for the planner or for sponsored products.

Social Media Integration:

- **Photo Booth:** Set up a themed photo booth where visitors can take pictures and are encouraged to tag your social media pages.
- **Live Social Media Updates:** Regularly update your social media with happenings at the expo, showcasing your booth and activities.

Networking and Partnerships:

- **Collaborate with Influencers:** If possible, invite influencers to your booth for meet-and-greet sessions.
- **Industry Networking:** Use this opportunity to connect with other exhibitors and attendees for future collaborations.

Workshops or Mini-Talks:

- **Educational Sessions:** Conduct short workshops or talks related to pregnancy, motherhood, and wellness, highlighting the usefulness of your planner in these journeys.

Follow-Up Strategy:

- **Newsletter Sign-Up:** Encourage visitors to sign up for your newsletter for future updates, tips, and offers.

- **Post-Expo Engagement:** Plan a post-expo email campaign for attendees who visited your booth, offering them exclusive content or discounts.

Remember, the key is to create an experience that's not only visually appealing but also emotionally resonant and practically valuable to your target audience. This approach not only promotes your planner but also strengthens the overall brand of Undefining Motherhood.

Just through one prompt to ChatGPT, Katy now has ideas she never even considered—like inviting influencers to her booth at a specific time and having stickers and markers to test out a planner. If Katy were to continue the conversation, she could write more prompts such as:

- Can you please design a plan for my booth? My trade show booth is 10' × 10'.
- What copy should I use on my signs to make my booth stand out?
- What topics should I do for my live Q&As that best align with my business goals?
- What are some cost-effective and high-quality vendors for branding merchandise in the US that I could use?
- Tell me more about a social media booth. What kind of technology would I need to rent or set up before the show?
- Give me some ideas for topics I could do when going live on social media at the trade show.
- Please identify some locally based influencers I could invite to my booth at the expo. Please also write a message I can send them introducing myself and asking if they're attending.

- Please detail a follow-up strategy for me that's as automated as possible so I don't lose any leads.
- I like all of these ideas. Can you please make a preproduction schedule and checklist to ensure I have everything ready to go seven days before the next expo starts on [Date of expo]? Today is [Today's date], and I can begin tasks next week. Please make this as detailed as possible so I can input the tasks into Undefining Motherhood's Asana.

It's easy to think of ChatGPT as a simple robot, but I assure you, the technology is anything but. Generative AI tools are fully capable of conversations, sometimes to the point where it feels like brainstorming with another human being. Use them to carry the mental load of planning your trade show appearance.

Write Effective Copy

What AI can do: Provide a solid first draft of campaign messaging.

Recommended AI tools for this task: Claude, Gemini, ChatGPT, Anyword

Data you might need on hand: Previous successful examples of your business's messaging, brand guidelines and tone of voice, target audience information, product or service details

You've read about artificial intelligence's abilities to analyze and interpret mass amounts of data—including behaviors like browsing and purchasing—for large and specific customer segments. When it comes to marketing messages, this ability can be used to analyze the effectiveness of your copy and make predictions about what will most resonate.

Even if you don't have an online store, you can still use artificial intelligence to help with your ad campaign. A generative AI tool—like Claude, Gemini, or ChatGPT—can also help you better understand the messaging that works best for your ideal customer.

You'll find no shortage of options if you Google artificial intelligence copywriting tools. Furthermore, you might consider exploring *There's An AI For That*, a website that is both self-proclaimed and widely regarded as the largest database of AI tools. Although its extensive collection can be overwhelming, it offers a comprehensive overview of the available AI solutions in the market. I recommend adopting a beginner's mindset and testing multiple tools to find the best fit for your needs and style.

Preferred Platform for Copywriting

To help you narrow down your search, here is my favorite tool:

- **Anyword.** Generating copy is one thing, but generating copy culturally sensitive to the current landscape is quite another. Anyword bucks this risk by generating copy that considers cultural trends and context. This results in copy that requires less editing by your team, ultimately saving everyone time and—on a somber note—a potential PR crisis. I like Anyword's Predictive Performance Score, which scores copy on its performance potential. This feature leverages historical data and AI to predict how well different versions of copy will perform, ensuring that your marketing messages are effective and resonant with your target audience.

Reach Customers Quickly with SMS Marketing

What AI can do: Draft personalized and timely texts to promote your business.

Recommended AI tools for this task: EZ Texting, SimpleTexting, Twilio, Textmagic, Klaviyo

Data you might need on hand: Customer phone numbers, customer preferences and purchase history, campaign goals and messaging

Text message marketing (SMS marketing) is an up-and-coming way to stay in touch with your customers. Instead of emailing, you can stay in touch through brief text messages. Given how often people are on their phones, this can be an effective and casual method to promote a sale or product, distribute an appointment reminder, or even check in to ensure service satisfaction. Artificial intelligence technology brings an unparalleled level of customization to SMS marketing. Instead of manually crafting customer text messages, AI can send hyper-personalized text messages instantaneously.

SMS marketing is an excellent communication tool, particularly when bolstered by artificial intelligence. Consider it for your small business if your ideal customers are one or more of the following:

- In leadership roles that have high inbox volumes.
- Under the age of forty.
- Potentially shopping at one or many competitors.

In essence, SMS marketing is like a shortcut into the pocket of your customer. Instead of getting in line with all the other emails, AI helps you share a brief update that matters to your customer. If you're unsure if SMS marketing is a good fit for your business, here's an example to help you evaluate.

AI in Practice

My client Judy Stakee has a fascinating career. As the former VP of Warner Chappell Music, she kick-started the songwriting careers of global forces like Sheryl Crow and Gavin DeGraw. Today, she is the founder and director of The Judy Stakee Company, the premier resource for songwriters serious about a music career. Through her company, Judy offers one-on-one coaching (on a selective basis) and hosts songwriting retreats worldwide. Her songwriting retreats are on an application basis, and she now has over seven hundred retreat alumni. She also has retreats that are for alums only.

Judy actively uses email marketing and social media and has developed an avid following online. However, the average age of a songwriting retreat attendee is midtwenties, meaning she might be able to connect with her current and future customers better via SMS marketing.

Here are the questions Judy could ask herself when evaluating SMS marketing for her business:

- **Do I want to develop a deeper interpersonal relationship with customers?** Judy's answer (and your answer) might vary for this question. Her email blasts get a lot of opens and clicks, but it's rare for her students to send an email to her personally. Therefore, there could be an opportunity for her to create more of an intimate experience with customers by using SMS marketing.
- **Do I have a lot of updates to share?** As a small business with frequent announcements on coaching spots, retreat applications, and overall educational guidance, Judy has a lot of updates to share with her list. When she sends more than one weekly email, she risks people unsubscribing, but at the same time, that weekly email can be lengthy. SMS marketing could be an effective and casual avenue to share small updates on her offerings without adding to inbox volume.
- **Do I want to add another communication method?** When Judy adds another communication method like SMS marketing, she needs to be prepared for replies from customers, particularly if artificial intelligence makes the texts personalized. While artificial intelligence can be trained to handle standard replies, there will be an inevitable training curve and partial management required from Judy and her team.

Here are some ways Judy can use SMS marketing.

Promoting Upcoming Retreats

If Judy sent a text without artificial intelligence to prospective songwriting retreat attendees, she might be inclined to write something like: "Join our songwriting retreat this summer. Great opportunity to learn and grow. Apply now! [Application link]"

But with artificial intelligence, the text could instead speak to that specific user: "Hi, [Name]! Ready to elevate your songwriting? I've got good news. Our next songwriting retreat in Nashville is open for application, and it's only a short flight away for you! Spots are filling up fast, so I recommend applying today. Reply if you need anything! [Application link]"

Notice how the second text addresses that Nashville is only a brief flight away from the attendee, who's addressed by first name. Those details will make the potential attendee feel valued and increase the likelihood of application.

Educational Reminders

Becoming a songwriter is ruthlessly competitive. It requires motivation, diligence, and a firm belief in the value of your creativity. I'm particularly excited about the possibility of Judy sending motivational texts to subscribers. Without AI, a text from Judy might look like this: "Don't forget to write every day. Keep your creativity flowing!"

But with artificial intelligence, here's what a subscriber could look forward to receiving: "Good morning, [Name]! As you head into your day, remember: A songwriter's journey never stops. Try to write down three song lines today. You never know what could become a masterpiece."

This text could be distributed at the morning hours of the recipient, ensuring they start their day with encouragement from Judy. It excites me to think about the brand loyalty that could potentially develop.

AI Tools for Text Messaging

Along with personalization (such as using the individual's name and other personal details), AI fortifies your message through language that strikes emotions and inspires a call to action. Plenty of AI tools are out there to help with this, but here are some favorites:

- **EZ Texting.** User-friendly and enhanced by artificial intelligence, EZ Texting is an SMS marketing tool tailored for small businesses' needs. Its intuitive interface is approachable, even for people who aren't tech savvy.
- **SimpleTexting.** SimpleTexting is a robust solution for small business owners. It's an accessible way to dive into SMS marketing and artificial intelligence.

- **Twilio.** For a more flexible platform, you might consider testing out Twilio. It's more advanced and allows for extensive personalization and integration. Like other platforms, Twilio can help business owners better understand customer patterns, ultimately enabling them to respond based on customer behavior.
- **Textmagic.** Textmagic is straightforward and effective. It's designed for small businesses that need a simple (but powerful) tool to reach customers. Textmagic can also manage large-scale messaging campaigns through its bulk SMS and auto-response features.

ALWAYS REVIEW AND REVISE AI-WRITTEN COPY

There's no doubt that AI tools are useful for data processing and automation. However, they can still capture human tendencies, including emotion, nuance, and language, which are the key ingredients for communicating with one another. Remember to use these remarkable tools to support the emotions, tones, and branding strategies you have created for your business. Let AI create a first draft of an email message, then review it to be sure it has your personal touch. Always be mindful of how AI can enhance your business, but remember that nothing will replace your opinion, experiences, and engagement as a small business owner.

Chapter 5

AI + Social Media and Content Creation

S mall business owners often get caught up in creating content and managing social media. This effort can be overwhelming and time consuming. I've witnessed several high-profile clients spend an unhealthy amount of time on their social channels, agonizing over every post like they're crafting a masterpiece. In most cases, it's not where they should focus their energy. The good news? AI is helping forge a new way of maintaining your brand's social media presence without losing sight of core business activities. This chapter will dive into how AI is revolutionizing how you approach social media and content creation, and you'll wonder how you ever managed your digital life without it.

HOW AI CAN HELP YOU WITH SOCIAL MEDIA

You already read how AI can assist with automating repetitive tasks, and social media is no different. You'll save time and generate ideas faster, which can foster more creativity and storytelling opportunities for your posts. At a high level, artificial intelligence can help you:

- Automate your content creation.
- Create your captions, posts, and basic graphics.

- Be consistent online through saved time and effort.
- Recognize content that will resonate with your followers.
- Increase your engagement on posts.
- Master visuals without hiring professional designers.
- Spot trends and topics.
- Understand who is in your audience and how to communicate with them.
- Post at the right time.
- Stay relevant and compete with larger companies' content.

PREFERRED PLATFORMS FOR SOCIAL MEDIA AND CONTENT

Here are some tools that can help you use social media even more effectively:

- **FeedHive.** FeedHive is a social media tool that uses several AI-powered features to improve users' content and boost engagement. The platform has an AI writing assistant, providing customized suggestions for post improvement and insights on the best time to post. It also offers a scoring tool to predict a post's performance and potential for virality. Users have the option to access AI-generated templated ideas for content creation. From creation to scheduling, FeedHive aims to streamline social media management and increase efficiency through AI and automation.
- **Brand24.** This tool is an all-seeing eye on the Internet, scanning data from news sites, blogs, and social media to reveal what's being talked about. For small businesses, these insights can be transformative, enhancing brand relevance and value. Brand24 captures sentiments, identifying customer service–related complaints and praises. It dives deep into specific market segments, which is valuable for businesses with specialized products or services. The tool provides alerts and reports on niche-relevant insights that are easily distributable to your team. Leveraging such data is crucial for improving customer service and effectively utilizing artificial intelligence.

- **Otis.** Otis's user-friendly interface makes it easy to get your social media campaign running quickly. Its AI analyzes the end destination of your ads—like a product listing or a sign-up page on your website—to create targeted ads that are likely to convert. It also optimizes and retargets your ads to maximize your ad spend.
- **NeuronWriter.** NeuronWriter creates high-quality, specific content to establish authority on topics for search engines and users alike. Its insights dive deep, showing which site pages need improvement, where users are spending time, and other important metrics relevant to your online presence. It also uses semantic models and search engine results page (SERP) analysis to optimize content for better ranking.
- **Revealbot.** Revealbot provides in-depth campaign analytics through AI technology while permitting marketers to maintain detailed control over their campaigns. This tool helps you establish customized automation and rules for your ad campaign for factors like bids, budget, and other criteria. It also integrates with Google Analytics to connect the dots between your campaign variables and user behavior on your website.
- **CoSchedule.** CoSchedule is a marketing platform that uses AI to help businesses organize, execute, and optimize their marketing efforts by automating workflows, improving content scheduling, and providing actionable insights. Its AI-driven features, like intelligent recommendations for social media posting times and content optimization, help small businesses enhance their marketing efficiency and reach more effectively.

Write Social Media Posts

What AI can do: Help you draft text using proven strategies and word choices.

Recommended AI tools for this task: Anyword, Adobe Express, FeedHive, Hootsuite, Buffer, CoSchedule, Sprout Social

Data you might need on hand: Social media account access, brand guidelines, engagement metrics, audience demographics, competitor analysis data

Crafting social media captions and long-form blog posts from scratch can be a daunting task. AI tools offer a starting point for content creation, sparking creativity. Many regular software platforms now have AI writing components built right in them. While these features may provide a solid foundation, it is important to incorporate storytelling, a unique brand voice, and individual perspectives to make content stand out on social feeds.

AI in Action

Try this prompt:

 Optimize this X post to go viral: [Copy and paste post].

AI excels at swiftly processing vast amounts of data to pinpoint content that has achieved exceptional success. By analyzing trends and engagement metrics, AI can uncover what resonates with audiences. Leveraging these insights, creators can strategically craft and position their own ideas to mirror proven successful patterns, enhancing the likelihood of their content's success.

Schedule Social Media Posts

What AI can do: Determine optimal posting times, provide suggestions for posting content to increase reach and engagement, and analyze engagement metrics for future content.

Recommended AI tools for this task: Adobe Express, Tailwind, Highperformr, Hootsuite, Lately, Buffer

Data you might need on hand: Social media account access, written content, brand guidelines, competitor analysis data, audience demographics

Whether you're a business of one or have a dedicated social media team, scheduling your content can be a game changer—especially when artificial intelligence is part of the software. In the days before AI, all social media was incredibly manual. Every post idea, design, hashtag, caption, and publishing act needed to be done step by step. Artificial intelligence now speeds up (and even improves!) content creation, and scheduling tools are no exception.

Instead of guessing the best day and time for your post to distribute, artificial intelligence tools can give you exact windows based on patterns of peak audience interactions. As opposed to manually calculating each post's performance, artificial intelligence in scheduling software creates hyper-precise reports. Some scheduling tools now suggest optimizations for your content before you hit "schedule," such as making text changes that will be more likely to resonate. Artificial intelligence is an additional brain to your social media efforts, helping you get better engagement faster.

Preferred Platforms for Scheduling Social Media Posts

These platforms are especially effective at this task:

- **Tailwind.** Tailwind describes itself as "your new marketing team" because it saves time for small businesses. The software allows you to schedule content for Pinterest, Facebook, and Instagram, so that you can release content at the time when your audience is most likely to engage. Outside of scheduling, Tailwind leverages artificial intelligence to also provide copywriting for fifty-plus functions, including ad copy, product listings, hashtag generation, and more.

- **Highperformr.** With a built-in AI coach, Highperformr helps you create and refine content for X (formerly Twitter) for more impact online. Their analytics can give you insight into daily, weekly, and monthly performance, and the tools have built-in automation to help free up your task list.

- **Adobe Express.** Adobe Express is useful as a social media content scheduler (in addition to other tasks). You can plan and create content within Adobe Express and schedule on TikTok, Instagram, Facebook, X (formerly Twitter), Pinterest, and LinkedIn. This integration simplifies your workflow by enabling you to design, plan, and schedule in one place.

- **Hootsuite.** Hootsuite began as a content scheduling tool, but now with artificial intelligence, it's a content creation tool as well. Hootsuite's OwlyWriter utilizes artificial intelligence to create post ideas, re-create the magic of your most successful posts without duplicating them, and create on-brand content for upcoming holidays. The software also analyzes your top-performing posts to determine the best scheduling times for your content.

- **Lately.** Lately's AI slices up long-form content to create short-form optimized social media posts that perform well. The AI studies your posts to create content that will get you maximum engagement. From there, you can schedule the content on Instagram, LinkedIn, Facebook, and X (formerly Twitter), and you can even set up approval workflows so that you can review the content before anything is distributed.

- **Buffer.** Buffer is a popular social media scheduling solution that has a plethora of data-driven tools, including its AI assistant, which can help creators generate new social media posts, repurpose existing ones, and come up with new ideas quickly. Buffer allows the content creator to gather more content ideas more quickly and spark more creativity.

Create and Enhance Images

What AI can do: Generate or enhance images quickly for marketing and branding purposes; provide design suggestions and templates tailored for specific needs and industries; and adjust image elements to fit various platforms and formats.

Recommended AI tools for this task: Adobe Express, Adobe Firefly, Adobe Photoshop, Lumen5

Data you might need on hand: Product or service images, brand guidelines, target audience data

A great way to use AI is for custom image creation or stylistic changes to art and photography. It's common practice for my clients to get new photos of themselves during a branding project, which might include an updated website, social media profiles, and other creative deliverables. A reshoot may be required if a client doesn't like certain elements of the final selected photos—background, outfit choice, or general environment—which also may come at the significant cost of rehiring a photographer. However, new AI features like generative fill in Adobe Photoshop have made adjusting these elements possible in a single click, saving both time and money for all involved. Here are three examples to show the power of generative fill.

Changing Backgrounds

My client Carey Thiels is a demand generation expert who helps B2B tech companies boost lead generation and hit revenue targets. Carey had a photoshoot to get lifestyle images for her website. Carey felt connected to a funky warehouse in downtown Boston; the exposed brick walls and minimalist furniture captured the no-fuss vibe of her brand. However, when Carey received her photos, she realized that the warehouse's red bricks didn't complement her brand's magenta and navy colors.

Thankfully, I knew about Adobe Photoshop's generative fill features. In a matter of seconds, the red bricks had a whitewash overlay. No reshoot required. Carey loved the photo so much that she made it the first image you see on her website's home page. Carey would have been looking at a reshoot costing her four figures if generative fill didn't exist.

Adding or Removing Objects

Photos with multiple team members can be challenging. One example is my work with Barstool Comforts, an online furniture store specializing in customizable barstools and dining chairs. Run by a mother-daughter duo, Deborah and Stephanie, I suggested getting photos of them for the website.

The photoshoot was a success. However, there was one photo in which Stephanie was pleased with how she looked in the photo, but Deborah was not. Stephanie wondered if there was a way we could crop the photo so she could still use it. Instead of cropping out Deborah, generative fill removed Deborah entirely. What's most remarkable about this example is that you'd never guess the photo has been tailored; it looks like Stephanie took it solo.

Think about how this might impact your next company team photo. Before artificial intelligence, companies either had regular group photos to account for attrition or favored solo headshots instead of group photos entirely. Now you can have group photos *and* easily remove people who no longer work in the company. Instead of having a shoot every quarter, companies can now have one every six months—or year.

Expanding Images

My client Rachel Melby is a Realtor and founder of Little Hill Real Estate. A key part of her brand identity design is text overlaid on images. Rachel got lifestyle photos taken for her new website. We received a stunning photo of Rachel that would be perfect for her website home page, except for one major issue: In the photo, Rachel is centered, so any text she added to her site would cover her face.

Since generative fill exists, this significant issue became a short hiccup with a quick resolution. We extended Rachel's image to the left (nearly doubling its width), so now Rachel appears on the right side of the image. We placed text on the left side, and it's legible because of the AI-generated background.

Create Videos and Live Streams

What AI can do: Livestream to multiple platforms simultaneously using various additional features.

Recommended AI tools for this task: Ecamm

Data you might need on hand: Product or service videos, brand guidelines, target audience data

If you are intimidated by the thought of creating video content or live streaming on social media, Ecamm might be your solution. The idea of producing video content can be overwhelming—crafting scripts, handling various gear, and filming yourself can feel like monumental tasks. The need for precise editing, ensuring high-quality audio and visuals, and maintaining an engaging presence on camera surely add to the pressure. This is where live streaming shines, as it requires minimal editing after the fact, making the process more straightforward and less time consuming.

Ecamm, an all-in-one video tool, allows you to live stream to YouTube, Facebook, LinkedIn, Instagram, Twitch, X (formerly Twitter), and other platforms simultaneously, simplifying your content creation process. It supports multiple cameras and screen sharing, and even has a built-in live camera switcher, making it easy to manage different views and presentations. Artificial intelligence enhances the tool by quickly recommending a video title the same moment you schedule your live stream. One less thing to worry about.

Stay On Top of Trends

What AI can do: Analyze market trends, provide insights into trending topics and keywords, and monitor competitors.

Recommended AI tools for this task: BuzzSumo, Google Trends, Brand24, Sprout Social

Data you might need on hand: Keywords and hashtags, competitor data, market research data

You've got a business to run, and you likely don't have hours in the day to dedicate to observing the next big social media trend. But if you want to grow on social media, you have to stay on top of trends. Trends can catapult your brand into popular conversations, demonstrate your unique perspective, and develop brand loyalty. Social media is like a cultural zeitgeist, and businesses that understand what's popular will generate a following (that, ideally, turns into customers).

Whether managing your social media on your own or employing a team to help, it can be challenging to spot trends—and know which ones are worth your time. Before artificial intelligence, trendspotting was a cumbersome process—one of ample research and time spent on various social platforms—but now by using AI, you can be aware of relevant trends and hashtags within seconds. You'll want to scan a wide net of content—social media posts, articles, and more—to identify topics with trend potential. The technology can also analyze which posts receive high engagement to inspire your business's content.

Preferred Platforms for Tracking Social Media Trends

These platforms are especially effective at this task:

- **BuzzSumo's** artificial intelligence applies predictive capabilities to identify spikes in specific topics, phrases, and hashtags poised to go viral, giving companies an edge to join the conversation before that topic takes off. It can also identify influential voices in particular industries, which can be advantageous for sponsored collaborations with creators.
- **Sprout Social's** AI takes monitoring a step further with sentiment analysis so that you can understand the opinions and moods of audiences from a high level.

Let's try using generative AI as a thought partner to better understand your audience's content expectations. Here's a prompt you can try.

Try a variation of this prompt:

 I own a wine store in Orlando, Florida. We specialize in New World wines, and we've been in business for thirty years. We want to revive our social media, and I need to understand better the type of content that will help our account grow. Can you please (1) highlight five to ten challenges my customers need solving by my business and (2) develop five to ten content topics for us?

 Certainly! Here are five to ten challenges that your customers may need solved by your wine store in Orlando, Florida:

1. **Wine Selection:** Customers may struggle with choosing the right wine for a particular occasion, meal, or personal preference.

2. **Wine Pairing:** Pairing wine with food can be challenging, so providing guidance on food and wine pairings can be helpful.

3. **Wine Education:** Many people want to learn more about wine, such as the different grape varieties, regions, and wine-making techniques.

4. **Gift Ideas:** Customers often seek recommendations for wine-related gifts for special occasions or holidays.

5. **Wine Tasting Tips:** Providing tips on how to properly taste and appreciate wine can enhance the overall experience.

6. **Wine Storage:** Guidance on how to store wine properly, especially in Florida's climate, is valuable.

7. **New Releases:** Informing customers about new arrivals and limited edition wines they can try or purchase is beneficial.

8. **Wine Events:** Promoting local wine events, tastings, and workshops can engage customers in the community.

9. **Wine Discounts and Promotions:** Sharing special discounts or promotions on select wines can attract budget-conscious customers.

10. **Wine and Health:** Exploring the health benefits of moderate wine consumption and its connection to well-being can be interesting.

Now, here are five to ten content topics for your social media accounts to address these challenges and engage your audience:

1. **"Wine of the Week":** Highlight a specific wine each week, sharing its tasting notes, pairing suggestions, and a special price for your followers.

2. **"Wine and Food Pairing Guides":** Create infographics or videos showcasing popular dishes paired with appropriate wines.

3. **"Wine 101 Series":** Offer short educational videos or blog posts about wine basics, such as grape varieties, regions, and terminology.

4. **"Gift Ideas for Every Occasion":** Share gift ideas, including wine sets, accessories, and personalized options, for birthdays, anniversaries, and holidays.

5. **"Wine Tasting Tips":** Post videos or articles on how to properly taste and evaluate wine, including information on aroma, taste, and finish.

6. **"Wine Storage Solutions":** Provide tips on storing wine at home, including temperature control and humidity management.

7. **"New Arrivals and Limited Editions":** Announce and showcase exciting new wines as they arrive in your store.

8. **"Local Wine Events":** Promote upcoming wine-related events in Orlando, whether they are at your store or in the area.

9. **"Flash Sales and Discounts":** Share time-sensitive promotions and discounts exclusively for your social media followers.

10. **"Wine and Health Benefits":** Explore the health benefits of moderate wine consumption and share interesting facts or studies on the topic.

By addressing these challenges and creating valuable content around these topics, you can revitalize your social media presence and engage your customers, ultimately helping your wine store grow.

Generate Business Names and Optimize Your Social Media Profiles

What AI can do: Suggest creative and relevant business names based on keywords and industry, as well as analyze and suggest improvements to your social media profiles.

Recommended AI tools for this task: Bing, Claude, ChatGPT, Namelix, Rytr, Copy.ai, Beacons.ai, Flodesk

Data you might need on hand: Business plan, target audience data, brand mission and values, a list of industry-specific keywords, existing social media profiles and analytics, competitor names for benchmarking

Would you attend a business meeting in a stained hoodie and oversized sweatpants? If you wanted to make a good first impression, you would put your best foot forward in your appearance. This same standard applies to your business's social media profiles, and artificial intelligence can help you dazzle any eyes that land on your accounts.

Choosing a Name

If you're new to business, figuring out your organization's name can be a major challenge. Luckily, the days of whiteboarding names are long gone, and you can now leverage artificial intelligence to create company names for you. Through its natural language processing abilities, artificial intelligence applies linguistics, trends, cultural considerations, and overall branding preferences to create business names.

Now, there is a caveat: Artificial intelligence is not a replacement for legal counsel, particularly regarding trademark and copyright. If AI comes up with a name that speaks to you, fantastic! But please do a quick trademark search to ensure no one owns the rights to that name before making anything official.

If you need a company name, I recommend a combination of tools: First, use a generative AI tool (like Bing, Claude, or ChatGPT), and then use Namelix. And, if you don't need a company name, you should still test out the following two tools in succession—simply to witness artificial intelligence in action.

AI in Action

Try a variation of this prompt:

 I am opening a car wash in San Diego, California. I need inspiration for a company name. Can you please provide me with a list of keywords for me to use in my brainstorming?

Certainly! For a car wash in San Diego, California, you might want to consider keywords that reflect the local vibe, the nature of your service, and anything unique about your approach. Here's a list to get your brainstorming started:

1. **Sunshine:** Reflecting the sunny weather in San Diego.

2. **Surf:** Nodding to the city's famous beaches and surf culture.

3. **Wave:** Symbolizing both the ocean and the motion of washing.

4. **Eco:** If your car wash is environmentally friendly.

5. **Pacific:** After the Pacific Ocean.

6. **SoCal:** Short for "Southern California," denoting the region.

7. **Bliss:** Suggesting a pleasing and effective car wash experience.

8. **Breeze:** Indicative of the coastal and easygoing lifestyle.

9. **Sparkle:** Signifying the end result of a clean car.

10. **Palm:** As a reference to palm trees and the Californian landscape.

11. **Crystal:** Indicating clarity and cleanliness.

12. **Shine:** The desired finish on a washed car.

13. **Coastal:** Denoting the coastal location of San Diego.

14. **Gleam:** A synonym for shine and gloss.

15. **Aqua:** For a water-related business.

16. **Marina:** Connecting to the city's boating and seaside culture.

17. **Oceanic:** Referring to the nearby ocean.

18. **Bay:** San Diego has many bays, which could be a good reference.

19. **Blue:** Representing both water and the clear skies.

20. **Suds:** Directly related to the soap and washing process.

These keywords can be combined or used as inspiration to create a unique and memorable name for your car wash.

Then, in Namelix, input the keywords, briefly describe the business, and see what comes up. The tool allows you to choose a name style. Here are a few great ideas for the San Diego car wash:

- Riptide Rinsers
- Soaksurf
- Surf Sparkle
- SoCal Spray
- Beachwashers
- Sunshine Soap
- San Diego Sparkle
- ZenWash
- Sunsoaked
- WashPacific
- And dozens of others

You can see how selecting a company name can also be helpful when considering social media. You can get an original name for your business and reserve those handles on social media for brand equity online.

Profile Photos

Your profile photo can make or break your first impression on social media channels, and artificial intelligence's image optimization abilities ensure you show up best on all platforms. Adobe Express is a top choice for image-driven AI tools. In a few clicks, you can remove your image background, resize your image, and more. This can be especially helpful for LinkedIn profile photos, where you can adjust your photo's background to fit nearly any aesthetic you'd like.

Profile Bio

When people come across any of your social media profiles, it's important that they can quickly understand your business's value and be incentivized to follow you on social media. In today's age, simply stating your business exists isn't enough. You need to articulate the value your content provides followers. Mastering this can be a tall order, especially considering each social platform has different character limitations in a bio field.

There are a few tools that can help with writing profile bios. You'll also find these tools are copywriting Swiss Army knives that can generate more content beyond bios. Remember the power of human minds collaborating with artificial intelligence when using them. The writing you receive might not be perfect, but that's okay—AI does the heavy lifting, and you can refine it.

Preferred Platforms for Profile Bios

Try these tools to assist with profile bios:

- **Rytr.** An all-in-one writing solution, Rytr harnesses artificial intelligence to generate copy with SEO in mind. Its AI-crafted bios can effectively capture a brand's essence, and you can choose the tone of voice that best suits your style.
- **Copy.ai.** Copy.ai is a powerful tool that generates a functional profile bio within minutes. Its AI technology understands each social platform's nuance and can tailor text accordingly.

Your Bio Link

Your bio link is critical to a social media profile, particularly on platforms like Instagram and TikTok that only allow one link. Artificial intelligence tools can automatically optimize the link in your bio to accommodate multiple links and opportunities for audience engagement.

Preferred Platforms for Bio Links

Here are some tools I recommend for bio links:

- **Beacons.ai.** There are plenty of link-in-bio services, but not many utilize artificial intelligence like Beacons.ai does. Beacons's AI enhances its service through functionality and intelligence, providing features like an online store, the ability to secure brand deals, and an email marketing strategy.
- **Flodesk.** Flodesk is celebrated for its visually appealing email templates and user-friendly design capabilities, which allow users to craft professional-looking emails effortlessly, as well as their link in bio. It stands out in the email marketing space with its streamlined workflow automation and segmentation (thanks to AI) and its cost-effective pricing plans, making it an excellent choice for creative professionals and small business owners alike.

Creating Channel-Specific Social Content

What AI can do: Curate effective content specific to a certain channel (e.g., Pinterest, Instagram, or YouTube) using that platform's best practices.

Recommended AI tools for this task: Lumen5, Agorapulse, InShot, VEED.io, Descript, Riverside, Circlebloom Publish, Pallyy, Mention, AISEO, FlexClip, Opus Clip, TrendTok, TubeBuddy, Movavi, Synthesia

Data you might need on hand: Social media account access, engagement metrics, audience demographics, brand guidelines, competitor analysis data, trending topics and keywords, previous content performance

Yes, artificial intelligence saves you time when creating social media posts. However, the exciting opportunity lies in artificial intelligence's ability to make social media posts *better*. AI's data processing capabilities far usurp standard human intelligence. It can generate content that will be effective based on thousands (or potentially millions) of data points related to human psychology.

Artificial intelligence is an unparalleled idea generator, capable of suggesting unique angles and ideas for content based on what's previously performed well for your business. It can help you stay relevant, fresh, and focused while staying true to your brand voice. I personally love generative AI as an instantaneous thesaurus (which I've even used to help me write this book!), providing ten to twenty variations to a word I might overuse.

Every social media platform has a unique culture and style, and artificial intelligence tools can help you instantaneously tailor content to fit each platform's best practices. Instead of posting the same content everywhere (which, frankly, disincentivizes users from following you on multiple platforms), artificial intelligence can adjust a single content idea to work within the norms of that particular platform. You might have one post idea, but with AI's involvement, you'll quickly have a unique piece of content for multiple social media channels.

Of course, there are some limitations to AI's social media generation abilities, which is where your discerning mind comes in. For example, artificial intelligence can fall short when understanding nuances of humor, often taking direction literally. But, again, editing and directing creative assets can be easier and faster than creating from scratch, so artificial intelligence is a no-brainer for creating first drafts of social media posts. Let's examine how you can maximize artificial intelligence for specific platforms.

Preferred Platforms for Pinterest

You've already read that Adobe Express is a trusted AI-powered tool for creating visuals, and it's an excellent resource for Pinterest. With a mouse click, Adobe Express creates polished graphics and templates to fit Pinterest's style requirements.

Pinterest is a search engine in its own right. The keywords you use in pins can be picked up by Google, augmenting your online discoverability. Writesonic's artificial intelligence technology helps you generate keyword-driven graphic text and pin captions to bolster user engagement. Here are some other options:

- **Lumen5.** Video content can be an effective format on Pinterest, and the AI of Lumen5 enables you to create compelling videos through its drag-and-drop interface. To save you time with manual searching, Lumen5 will suggest related images and video clips based on your provided text, which frees you up to focus on designing a video that's true to your brand.

- **Agorapulse.** Agorapulse is noteworthy for its comprehensive social media management capabilities. Agorapulse's platform offers insightful analytics and scheduling features, making it easier to manage Pinterest content alongside other social media channels. This integration allows for a cohesive strategy that enhances your brand's presence across platforms, leveraging AI to ensure your Pinterest strategy is as efficient and engaging as possible.

Preferred Platforms for Instagram

On Instagram, you can post videos, photos, and graphics—and artificial intelligence can support you with all formats. Without artificial intelligence, video editing can be costly in terms of time and effort. If you're on a budget, you might painstakingly edit video content independently, even though you have a business to run. And if you invest in a video editor, it can sometimes take hours to edit a single video. Multiple artificial intelligence tools replace the need for a video editor, including Lumen5. Here are some other options:

- **InShot.** InShot is a popular video editing app where you can create professional content from your phone. The app employs AI technology to improve footage and apply effects. For example, the AI can apply presets to improve your video's appearance, automatically transcribe speech in video captions, remove backgrounds, and smooth out slow-motion effects for better quality.

- **VEED.io.** VEED.io's app offers a wealth of features that greatly assist businesses in video creation. The app enables the creation of unique virtual avatars, serving as digital spokespersons for your business. Additionally, it allows for the generation of custom images, ideal for use as thumbnails in Reels, and supports the creation of voice-overs in multiple languages. A standout feature of the app is its innovative eye contact technology, where artificial intelligence adjusts the speaker's eye direction to maintain consistent eye contact with the camera, enhancing viewer engagement.

- **Descript.** Descript is a versatile content creation tool used by millions of creators. It transcribes and edits audio and video by text, removes filler words, adds captions and graphics, and generates SEO-friendly blog posts. Its "Underlord" AI features streamline podcast editing and video production.

- **Riverside.** Riverside has introduced AI tools that focus on creating high-quality recorded content. These features include text-based video editing, AI-driven clip selection for short-form content, noise reduction, real-time audio leveling, podcast show notes creation, and automatic transcription for seamless post-production.

If you need help with writing Instagram captions, multiple tools employ generative AI and natural language processing technology. These tools can create high-quality and engaging captions, and many of the tools can adjust the captions to fit your brand's written tone of voice:

- **Circlebloom Publish.** Circlebloom has multiple products, and you'll want to check out this one for support with copywriting. It's powered by OpenAI (the technology behind ChatGPT) to generate captions and source hashtags for any post you create. This intuitive tool works for Instagram, X (formerly Twitter), Facebook,

LinkedIn, and Pinterest to have an all-in-one solution for multiple channels.

- **Pallyy.** An affordable AI solution, Pallyy is a social media management platform incorporating AI technology like image caption and image description generation. Pallyy uses advanced language models and algorithms to write captions with nuance—zeroing in on your post's topic and mood. It also works for multiple platforms and has a scheduler.

- **Mention.** Mention combines content creation, publishing, and monitoring into one AI-powered platform. It has features like username, caption, hashtag, and bio generation for Instagram, and it monitors media mentions and brand perception to inform content decisions.

- **AISEO.** AISEO is a multipurpose generative AI and natural language processing tool specializing in content generation. It creates short- and long-term content that aligns with your brand's SEO goals. A quick note that the tool doesn't specialize in Instagram per se, but if you want one platform to tackle blog posts and short-form content, this could be a sufficient solution that cuts back on multiple subscriptions.

Preferred Platforms for TikTok

TikTok videos might be short, but the many steps required to create content behind the scenes can be burdensome for even the savviest marketers. AI tools can give you a leg up with efficiency by automating repetitive tasks, optimizing your content, and even potentially making your video edits a higher quality than humans can. Here are some tools that can help:

- **FlexClip.** FlexClip is an online tool that makes it easy to create branded video content. It features multiple templates, including ones for TikTok, giving you a jump start in video content. It boasts a royalty-free music library (a solution to a challenge commonly faced by companies on TikTok) and features AI capabilities like video scripting, caption generation, background remover, and more.

- **Opus Clip.** If you have long-form content like keynote speeches to convert into TikTok-friendly clips, Opus Clip's AI technology excels at this. It trims long videos into shorter content for TikTok, Instagram, and YouTube Shorts. The AI identifies key moments, adds animated captions automatically, and enhances engagement with AI-generated B-roll and custom templates.
- **TrendTok.** TrendTok utilizes AI to find viral trends, including music. You can filter the trends based on your account category (industry or topics) and location. Within the TrendTok app, you can save trending sounds, which will help you stay a few steps ahead with content creation. It also leverages predictive analytics to forecast the next big sound.

Preferred Platforms for YouTube

As a search engine owned by Google, YouTube can be a powerful force for generating SEO value and driving site traffic. I've experienced the benefits of YouTube with my digital footprint. After you learn about some AI tools, I will give a quick overview of my personal journey and how YouTube has unleashed a business vertical that now comprises 20% of my company revenues:

- **TubeBuddy.** TubeBuddy is a great tool for optimizing YouTube videos. It's both a browser extension and mobile app that gives you a potential YouTube title and a score based on SEO potential. It also includes keyword recommendations, thumbnail analysis, and title generation.
- **Movavi.** Movavi's video editor uses AI technology to help businesses elevate their video content—with or without an editor. Through their intuitive platform, you can remove backgrounds, change backgrounds, add motion tracking, apply an audio denoiser, and more. What would take a video editor hours to do

manually can be done almost instantly, and you don't need to be a video editor to harness this technology.

- **Synthesia.** Synthesia creates AI avatars that can be replicas of you or chosen from one of the 140+ natural avatars. From there, those avatars can read aloud scripts, acting as TV hosts, in over 120 different languages. The tool is intuitive, and the technology itself is a marvel.

Respond to Direct Messages

What AI can do: Respond to customer messages automatically and provide immediate responses.

Recommended AI tools for this task: Manychat, Intercom, Zendesk, Customers.ai, Chatfuel

Data you might need on hand: Social media account access

Many small businesses think of social media as a broadcasting tool, which is false: It's a relationship-building tool. Creating and scheduling content is only part of the equation for a successful social media presence. After intriguing prospective and current customers with content, we business owners must nurture those relationships with community management.

It's not always realistic or practical to reply to every comment or DM you receive, particularly if your company is on multiple social media platforms. While artificial intelligence can't entirely handle all communication attempts, it can certainly deal with a high volume of basic questions, which is where AI chatbot tools come into play. This book has already recommended Manychat, so here are a few others:

- **Intercom.** Intercom provides comprehensive customer support solutions, including AI-driven chatbots that can handle inquiries on social media. It integrates with various platforms like Instagram, Facebook, email, and SMS, allowing for automated responses to common questions and freeing up your team to focus on more complex interactions.

- **Zendesk.** Zendesk offers robust customer service tools, including AI-powered chatbots that can manage social media inquiries efficiently. It helps automate repetitive tasks and provides quick responses to frequently asked questions, thus ensuring no customer query goes unanswered.
- **Customers.ai.** Ranked highly for its versatile chatbot functionalities, Customers.ai enables automated yet personalized interactions on Messenger, native web chat, and SMS. It's beneficial for creating conversational marketing campaigns and customer service bots.
- **Chatfuel.** Chatfuel specializes in automating responses and engaging users on Facebook. It offers an intuitive interface for creating AI-driven chatbots, enhancing interaction quality on social media pages.

Track Analytics

What AI can do: Track, manage, and analyze your social media performance.

Recommended AI tools for this task: Sprout Social, Whatagraph

Data you might need on hand: Social media account access, engagement metrics, audience demographics, previous content performance, competitor analysis data

There's a saying I love: "Without data, you're just another person with an opinion." Data can be the difference between making significant sales or being a blip on someone's radar in social media and content creation. In the initial days of social media, analytics was a heavily manual world—requiring CSV exports, time-consuming calculations, and a human to interpret the findings. With artificial intelligence tools, you save work hours, energy, and the risk of human error when calculating your social media. Instead of trying to decipher engagement rates and follower growth rates, AI tools instantly figure that out for you.

Data for Social Media

Data in social media can be dense and overwhelming. Typically, every social media channel has three main groupings of data: post-level, page-level, and audience behavior. With post-level analytics, you're determining the performance of a specific post. With page-level, you'll be assessing the cumulative impact of your pieces of content to determine your account's overarching reach and growth. From an audience standpoint, most social media platforms can break down who's engaging with your content, starting with their age, gender, and location and, on certain platforms, drilling down into interests, education, marital status, and more.

From a content creation standpoint, having data on your posts is critical. Not only can you observe what your audience responds to; you can also glean extra insight—such as if the algorithm is currently favoring videos, links, or photos—and adjust your content accordingly. Once you employ artificial intelligence technology, you'll immediately have objective insights into your content, and it will likely be more accurate, timely, and actionable than a human's interpretation.

While the end goal for many businesses posting on social media is, generally, sales, audience growth can be a critical vehicle for expanding your brand's digital presence. Ideally, your posts are helping you grow in followers, and artificial technology can help you track growth—or pinpoint why it's not happening.

Understanding Content Performance

The following tools use machine learning and ultrafast data processing to identify patterns and trends in your post performance and, in essence, tell you why a post is or isn't doing well. This information is critical so you and your social media associates can do more of what is working—and grow.

My favorite AI tool for content performance is Sprout Social. Also a scheduling platform, Sprout Social incorporates artificial intelligence to bring clarity to users in a variety of ways, including:

- Aggregating data across various platforms so you understand how campaigns are doing.
- Identifying the individual performance of each post in comparison to other content pieces.
- Determining trends in audience behavior.
- Analyzing and segmenting your audience based on behavior, allowing you to tailor your content strategy accordingly.
- Predicting the best times to post based on previous high engagement.
- Examining your post text, visuals, and video to identify trends and suggest improvements.
- Understanding overall sentiment behind your comments from users using natural language processing.
- Benchmarking your competitors to garner insights into their potential strategies.
- Surfacing broader market trends that may be of relevance to your brand.
- Generating reports at set intervals so you always have insight into channels.

The information will empower your social media creators to make decisions based on data without the mental load of data interpretation.

Understand Your Audience

What AI can do: Analyze engagement metrics, track audience behavior, and provide content recommendations.

Recommended AI tools for this task: Sprout Social, Agorapulse, Emplifi, Audiense

Data you might need on hand: Engagement metrics, audience demographics, content performance history, social media platform analytics

Social media wasn't originally designed for businesses. It was created to connect people. While we're far away from only being able to use Facebook with a college email address, the foundational principles remain the same: When you post on social media as a business, your content competes with friends and family as much as other businesses.

Users today are very discerning, and the more you can make them feel part of a community, the more they will pay attention. Artificial intelligence tools can help you understand your social media followers with extreme detail, further creating opportunities for your brand to connect with individuals.

There are several tools you can use to delve deeper into your audience. In addition to Sprout Social, consider exploring Agorapulse (mentioned earlier), Emplifi, or Audiense. Each of these tools can assist you to:

- Stay up-to-date on audience needs and behaviors, allowing you to be agile and adjust your marketing strategy accordingly.
- Predict content performance and audience preferences.
- Get distilled information on the type of content your audience prefers to help you create more of what's working well.

Identify Beneficial Content Creator Partnership Opportunities

What AI can do: Review potential partners and suggest choices that are a good fit for your business.

Recommended AI tools for this task: BuzzSumo, HypeAuditor, Klear, AspireIQ, CreatorIQ

Data you might need on hand: Brand values and campaign goals, target audience demographics, engagement metrics, available budget and resources

Word of mouth might be the best form of advertising, but creator partnerships may be the second-best thing. If you want your business to stand out on social media, hiring an influencer to do a sponsored content post might be what your business needs to take off online.

As a content creator myself, I've partnered with hundreds of brands to test and share their product with my community. A successful partnership benefits both sides: For me, it means promoting tools or services that offer real solutions to business owners at a fair price. For the companies I collaborate with, it involves partnering with a creator who consistently produces engaging content that appeals to their target audience.

If you're considering hiring a content creator, there are many important factors to review:

- **Do they create content that aligns with how you want your product or service portrayed?** For example, if a creator is known for being crass or comedic, this could be a nightmare or a dream come true, depending on your company's values.
- **Are they reliable and trustworthy?** To determine this, you might want to know if they've done successful partnerships.
- **Are you comfortable with them being honest about your product or service?** A creator's job is to be honest with their followers. They might share that they don't love everything about your product.
- **Do you have a certain budget in mind?** You might be surprised by how much creators charge for content partnerships, so it's important to know what budget you'd like to stay within, especially since a creator can't guarantee sales results.
- **Do you want to own the final photo or video files?** Unless specified in a contract, copyright is automatically assigned for any creator's content, so you'd need to either pay for ownership (which some creators won't agree to) or license the photos or videos for advertising or other use.

And that's just the tip of the iceberg. You can imagine how overwhelming influencer partnerships can be on both sides. The social media landscape can seem like the Wild West, and each partner often has different (and sometimes conflicting) goals. Artificial intelligence can help reduce overwhelm, ensuring successful partnerships where both parties are a good match.

Preferred Platforms for Finding Partnerships

With millions of creators out there, artificial intelligence can act as your filter and hiring manager, serving up the creators that best align with your goals:

- **BuzzSumo.** BuzzSumo's predictive AI technology can help identify trends, but it also boasts an entire *database* of influencers across multiple social media platforms. You can filter within this database—like audience demographics, creator's location, ideal engagement rates, and more—to find a creator who best aligns with your product or service.

- **HypeAuditor.** If you're worried about the smoke and mirrors of social media, give HypeAuditor a go. This artificial intelligence tool focuses on authenticity by analyzing a creator's profile and engagement. The tool will tell you if it suspects a creator has bought followers, and it will also make sure the creator has adhered to advertising regulations in previous partnerships. Even better, HypeAuditor's predictive technology can predict an influencer's campaign performance, helping you find peace of mind before entering a partnership.

- **Klear.** Meltwater's Klear describes itself as an "influencer marketing platform" that connects brands and businesses. The app uses artificial intelligence to help companies find influencers that match their requirements. Klear's AI technology categorizes influencers into specific groupings (from nano to mega influencers) and analyzes engagement levels.

- **AspireIQ.** AspireIQ is an influencer CRM and content marketing platform. Like the other platforms, AspireIQ helps you locate influencers through AI technology that predicts campaign success. After matching with the influencer, AspireIQ uses artificial intelligence to automate workflows, such as assigning campaign briefs, approvals, and even media licensing. After the campaign runs, AI capabilities measure the return on investment of the influencer campaign, which can help drive future business decisions.

- **CreatorIQ.** This AI-powered tool brings advanced data and reporting to small businesses in the creator economy, helping to demystify the process and return on investment. Its built-in search engine drills into hyper-specific creator categories, allowing you to find and vet creators quickly. You can also use the platform to analyze community trends, to execute and manage creator campaign activations, and, with its robust reporting capabilities, to anticipate your program performance.

Create Search Engine–Optimized Content and Run Paid Social Media Campaigns

What AI can do: Check trends, manage budgets, and decide which campaigns deserve a paid strategy.

Recommended AI tools for this task: Otis, Revealbot

Data you might need on hand: Campaign performance metrics, ad spend data, audience demographics, market trends and insights, content performance data, sales and conversion data, keyword research data

If you maximize every part of your organic social media strategy and still desire more exposure, paid social media ads could be a smart move for your business. Social media ads give you creative flexibility—including videos, carousels, and stories—and ultraprecise targeting to help your ads reach your most desired audience. But, while social media campaigns are quick to set up and launch, they're not for the faint of heart. One ad mistake can have significant consequences for your business, be it a lost budget, a missed conversion opportunity, or even risking your reputation. Artificial intelligence tools reduce risk when running ad campaigns. Here are some of the many benefits:

- The AI algorithm can augment social media ads' targeting with even more precision. It can analyze large quantities of data from your website, including sales trends, and even from the social campaigns themselves to determine the optimal user segments for your campaign. This, in turn, helps with your ads' relevance and overall effectiveness.

- AI's machine learning and data analytics algorithms can help you manage budgets across multiple platforms. Instead of manually keeping track of what money is spent where, AI can adjust and manage your budgets simultaneously based on metrics such as click-through rate (CTR), cost per acquisition (CPA), and overall engagement. You can imagine how useful this would be if there were a quick and drastic change in market conditions; AI could sense a change in your advertising campaign effectiveness and allocate your budget accordingly.

- AI's data processing capabilities are ongoing, and the more information it has, the better results you can receive. Like finding pieces of a puzzle, artificial intelligence gleans more insights as your campaign progresses, making it even more efficient with predicting successful ads and targeting over time.

- Before artificial intelligence, every campaign required manual management. If you wanted to scale your efforts, your social media campaign manager would need to work longer, or you'd have to expand your team. This isn't the case anymore with artificial intelligence tools. With AI doing the heavy lifting of targeting, budget management, and even generating creative content, your small business will be better positioned to scale up its paid marketing efforts.

Chapter 6

AI + Customer Service

W

e've all been there: Your flight is canceled, or an order is incorrect, and you must make a dreaded customer service call. Instead of speaking with a representative right away, you must listen to elevator music for hours, and your entire day is halted. When you finally get to speak to a representative, you're (understandably) irritable. If the problem isn't resolved, you'll likely avoid purchasing from that business again.

The quality of a customer service experience can be the difference between customers becoming more loyal or never buying from you again. As your business grows, you need to hire more trained staff, and maintaining quality can be difficult with a growing team. Beyond that, hiring might not always be the most cost-effective solution, particularly if you're a seasonal business. This chapter will review how artificial intelligence can help you expedite and scale your business's customer service without compromising the experience.

TECHNOLOGY IN CUSTOMER SERVICE BEFORE AI

Interactive voice response (also known as IVR) predates artificial intelligence as a technology solution in customer service that reduced the need for a human representative. In IVR, an automated voice guides you through a series of prompts to get you to the right type of representative.

No doubt you have had this experience when calling your bank. The IVR technology can be frustrating; these systems attempt a one-size-fits-all approach, but if you have a specific need, the scripted set of options might not apply to you.

Another example of pre-AI customer service includes email support systems. I don't know about you, but I don't respond well to receiving a templated email reply that doesn't address my question or concerns. As a customer, few things are more exasperating than not feeling heard, and poor customer service emails are a perfect example of this in action.

Scaling your customer service division pre-AI was also a huge endeavor from a business owner's perspective. Critical data might be siloed in different places within your organization—like sales records being separate from your customer service notes—making it hard for customer service representatives to understand a customer's full history with your company. Overall, older systems lacked the nuance to merge data and language for a truly customized customer service experience.

ACCEPTING CUSTOMERS' HIGH EXPECTATIONS

An article on customer service by McKinsey & Company shared a staggering conclusion: 75% of online customers expect help within 5 minutes. *Five* minutes! Meeting that demand would be nearly impossible for most businesses unless multiple people worked 24-hour shifts. Adding to the urgency: This article was published in 2016, meaning customers might expect help even faster today. Additionally, Document360 conducted their own survey in 2023 that found 75% of customers expect brands to offer 24/7 customer service. Both conclusions underscore why artificial intelligence isn't just an aspiration for small businesses; it's necessary to satisfy your customers.

Not only is speed a requirement (as far as customers are concerned); the quality of the customer service experience is also paramount. A recent Zendesk Customer Experience Trends Report found that 74% of customers feel loyal to a brand or company, where price ranks first as a contributing factor and service is a close second. This finding underscores how excellent customer service acts as a critical tool for retention, loyalty, and repeat sales. Good customer service can ensure customers' continued patronage and investment in a brand.

Without artificial intelligence, your business's customer service function may unintentionally erode trust and amplify customer dissatisfaction. If you reply too slowly, statistics suggest they'll be displeased. If you use IVR technology, they may be frustrated by a cookie-cutter approach to their issue. If you use email templates, they may feel like they're just a number instead of a valued customer. If your customer sales representative can't access their sales history, the customer may feel unimportant. And if the customer service experience doesn't go well, your business will leave potential money on the table.

In short, the risks of maintaining the status quo for customer service are high. Artificial intelligence tools can mitigate those risks. Let's review how to apply this technology to your business.

THE BENEFITS OF USING AI IN CUSTOMER SERVICE

When you bring artificial intelligence into your customer service efforts, you can surpass standard FAQs and deliver a truly personalized experience. Thanks to artificial intelligence's natural language processing and data capabilities, your customers can receive communications adjusted to suit their past behaviors, expressed issue(s), and preferences. As you've seen in previous chapters, AI's superpower lies in its ability to continuously learn, which means it will continue to improve to be more helpful and more satisfactory for your customers.

Personalization

Artificial intelligence brings a seemingly human touch to customer interactions. It can make interactions more personalized by greeting based on the time of day ("Good morning, Dave!"), referencing a product or service they recently purchased ("How are you enjoying your vitamin C serum?"), and adding other small touches to improve the interaction. Interestingly, AI can enhance customers' shopping experiences, even if they initially reach out for an issue. After a customer is satisfied, your artificial intelligence tool can suggest products or services directly aligned with the individual's purchase history and communications with your company.

Ability to Escalate Certain Cases to a Human

An important consideration: Artificial intelligence's capacity for providing personalized customer service experiences still has limitations, and this is where human interactions come in. For example, imagine scaling your customer interactions to have hundreds or thousands of completely customized conversations happening simultaneously, with language to suit the customer's communication needs and conversation points that speak to their history with your company. With artificial intelligence as the first touchpoint in your business, customers will get their problems solved faster and, potentially, better—and your human customer service representatives can step in if a situation is beyond AI's expertise. If your AI faces a particularly disgruntled customer or a query it's unsure about, the AI will escalate the case to your human representative, along with notes, so the customer doesn't need to repeat information. This scenario demonstrates a perfect synergy between AI and human interaction. By allowing AI to handle routine inquiries and optimize operational efficiency, human agents can focus on more layered issues that benefit from personal connection.

Saving You Time

Addressing customer questions and concerns as a human agent is anything but easy. The customer may always be right, but those customers can still require a lot of time. A seemingly quick query from a client can take you 15–20 minutes in which to reply. Multiply that by twelve clients, and you've spent half of your workday answering questions instead of doing work that propels your business forward.

This is one of the many reasons artificial intelligence is essential for any business wanting to scale. I'd go so far as to say that, out of all the chapters in this book, implementing AI into your customer service vertical is the most important.

Here are some of the possible downsides for your business that you might face if you do not add an AI interface to your customer experience.

If you're a one-person business:

- You might be held back from more important priorities, like providing services, designing products, planning your year, pursuing education, and more.
- You might struggle to keep up with email volume and complexity of inquiries, leading to dissatisfied customers and, potentially, missed sales opportunities if your inbox is overflowing.
- You won't have a backup, meaning if you have a personal emergency, get called away during peak times, or even get sick, every inquiry will have to wait until you're back and able to work.
- You might not be as good at customer service as you think, and these skill gaps could cost you without your knowledge.

If you're a multi-person business:

- Your customer service experience could suffer because of the increase in number and range of queries that require more knowledge from your human agents.
- You might find it challenging to train a larger team to adhere to your high standards.
- You might face more and more data issues, particularly across departments (like sales and billing), with a higher volume, which affects the knowledge your representatives can access about the customer.
- Your team might burn out with the repetitive nature of customer service tasks, particularly if they're on calls daily.
- You might have high costs to update your technology, merge data across departments, and expand your team with competent representatives.

Needless to say, customer service can be an exhausting job, both for the people doing it and for the business owners who are managing teams. Artificial intelligence can reduce the workload of human agents by taking over routine tasks and queries, which can help human workers focus on their strengths, thereby working strategically to improve the customers' experiences with the company.

PREFERRED PLATFORMS FOR CUSTOMER SERVICE

I mentioned Intercom and Zendesk earlier. Beyond those, here are a few more customer service tools worth checking out:

- **Ada.** Ada's website describes the tool as "a full customer service team, powered by AI." Notable businesses have employed Ada as a website chatbot, and its chat capabilities work in more than fifty different languages. In addition to its standard chatbot, Ada has voice AI capabilities to handle phone calls too. Using human-level reasoning, Ada can be coached to understand the language your company would use with customers, how you'd handle support tickets, and anything else that aligns with your company's policies.
- **HappyFox.** HappyFox is a conversation-led customer service tool that can categorize and assign support requests, particularly in HR and IT. The tool consolidates tickets from different channels (like social media, phone, email, and chats) so the customer's issue can be resolved no matter how they communicate with your business. It has a user-friendly interface that makes it easy for your team to leaf through tickets and set up customizable workflows.
- **Freshdesk.** Freshdesk uses AI technology to help small businesses manage, prioritize, and resolve customer service requests. It includes a scalable knowledge base that helps your customers quickly find answers, and it improves team productivity and efficiency through AI-powered automation. The tool leverages generative AI to assist agents as well by providing insights in real time when dealing with a customer.

- **Kustomer.** An AI-powered customer service CRM, Kustomer connects multiple customer service touchpoints—social media, email, WhatsApp, phone, and more—to create a centralized database for your agents. With a chatbot feature and quick access to FAQs, SMS, and voice capabilities, Kustomer tracks data at every step to see improvement opportunities.

- **Gorgias.** Designed for e-commerce like Shopify, WooCommerce, Magento, and BigCommerce, Gorgias provides 24/7 customer support and helps your business in gathering comprehensive data points. You can get information on a customer's loyalty status, order history, and more to enhance personalized replies from human agents.

- **LivePerson.** LivePerson takes pride in providing authentic customer conversations through its AI-powered technology. The tool leads to an average 30% reduction in operating costs and a 25% boost in customer satisfaction. LivePerson integrates with Salesforce, Microsoft Dynamics, NetSuite, SugarCRM, WhatsApp, and more, allowing you to connect and uncover data across multiple platforms.

- **Gladly.** Gladly's AI technology organizes customer service queries by customers, not tickets. As a ticket-free solution, Gladly delivers a completely personalized customer experience by drawing from that customer's purchasing history, behavior, and loyalty status. Whether over SMS, voice, or email, every customer contact is unified into a single conversation view, making it easy for both AI and human agents to understand the customer.

- **Sprout Social.** Sprout Social's social media monitoring and engagement tools help businesses track and respond to customer feedback across various platforms. Its AI-driven analytics provide insights into customer sentiment and trends, enabling your team to tailor responses and improve customer satisfaction. By consolidating social media interactions, Sprout Social ensures no customer comment goes unnoticed, which helps maintain a positive brand image and efficient customer service.

Reduce Repetitive Tasks

What AI can do: Free up human time by responding to simple customer questions, personalizing its response as needed.

Recommended AI tools for this task: Manychat, Zendesk, Intercom, Customers.ai

Data you might need on hand: Common questions and their corresponding answers, customer interaction history, product or service information, brand guidelines and tone of voice

We've reviewed how chatbots can be beneficial for amplifying your touchpoints for business sales, but chatbots can also be extremely beneficial as the first line of defense for basic customer service issues and questions. Through natural language processing and machine learning technologies, artificial intelligence can adjust its tone and topics in real time to fit the communication needs of your customer. These tools allow for instantaneous responses so your human agents can be freed up to handle more complex and serious issues.

Consider seeking a chatbot that can be a solution for both your sales and your customer service needs. As mentioned earlier, Manychat is a sales tool that could double up for customer service as well. This AI tool can answer routine customer inquiries right from your website in the form of a chatbot.

Triage Help Tickets

What AI can do: Determine which requests are top priority.

Recommended AI tools for this task: Zendesk, Intercom, Freshdesk

Data you might need on hand: Ticket details, customer information, historical ticket data, categorization criteria

Without a ticket triage system, it can be hard to know what customer service issues to tackle first. Often you may find yourself wanting to solve issues of clients who are the "loudest" instead of focusing on which issue is the most important—and it can be a slippery slope.

When you merge artificial intelligence into your customer ticketing systems, AI will automatically prioritize tasks for you and your team with the most pressing issues first. Instead of jumping from task to task, your human agents will know exactly what to resolve first with no guesswork.

The benefits of including artificial intelligence in your ticketing system include:

- Improved response times by focusing your team on resolving tasks instead of putting their efforts into determining the order in which tasks should be completed.
- Increased efficiency by directing tickets to the proper agent or department with consideration to the type of issue.
- Better data insights on your customer service to improve your systems, flesh out your FAQs, expand your chatbot responses, fix your products, or even expand your team based on the most frequently recurring issues, peak support times, and performance of your human agents.

Artificial intelligence's role in your ticket triage systems can vary depending on your needs and the technology you use. At a foundational level, artificial intelligence sorts and prioritizes requests through natural language processing by deciphering the topic of the customer complaint and then distributing it among your agents accordingly. It can also consider a customer's status or history with your company as a factor when prioritizing so that you can get to long-standing customers quickly.

Depending on the AI system you use, some tools can partially resolve tickets of a simpler nature, like password resets and order tracking. Your customer service team will save time by not being involved with the request, but they'll also save mental bandwidth by not even having to *think* about the request and its level of priority among the other tickets in the queue.

Get Insights about Your Customer Service

What AI can do: Improve your customer service and overall business by getting data about your customers' needs, issues, and behaviors.

Recommended AI tools for this task: Zendesk, Intercom, Manychat, Kustomer, Gorgias, LivePerson, Gladly, Sprout Social

Data you might need on hand: Customer interaction logs, customer feedback and survey data, support ticket history, agent performance metrics, customer demographics

When you incorporate artificial intelligence into your customer service, it's like a data-absorbing fly on the wall with every interaction. You'll be able to glean real-time insights about your customers, and the artificial intelligence technology can make suggestions regarding actions for agents and task automation to increase efficiency. Some tools will even provide detailed sentiment analysis on customer interactions so you can better comprehend your customers' emotions and your agents' performances. Some of the many benefits of using AI chatbots to get data about your customer service include:

- Getting a better understanding of your customers. AI chatbots can extract data from seemingly unquantifiable human interactions. That information can help you objectively grasp your customers' behaviors and patterns when interacting with your business.
- Understanding the different segments you serve. You might know one customer type well, but multiple segments could interact with your business. Data extracted by artificial intelligence can help you uncover different customer types in great detail—their needs, issues, and behaviors—so your business can create the best experience possible for that segment.
- Pinpointing common friction points or issue areas. AI chatbots can extensively analyze your customer service conversations to isolate frequent questions or issues, empowering your team to make changes for even more efficiency.

- Isolating the exact time to solve customer service issues so you can repair systems or staff your team accordingly.
- Highlighting your superstar agents! Many AI chatbots can give you insights into human agent performance and areas of potential improvement to figure out who's earned more responsibilities and who needs more training.
- Holistically understanding your customer journey, including your business's various touchpoints across channels and, importantly, how much your customers like those interactions.

With this level of insight, you and your customer service team could create meaningful solutions in particular parts of your business. If you learn about a specific issue or area of confusion in a service, you could adjust your onboarding instructions to provide information that is clearer. If there's a tone of voice that a specific customer segment best responds to, your human agents could be trained to speak in that tone. Your team's quality of life will improve by having these repetitive tasks automated, and you'll be more poised to work *on* the business instead of *for* the business.

AI IN PRACTICE

My client Simon T. Bailey is an award-winning motivational speaker. He often does over one hundred speaking engagements annually to conferences and corporations, and he's worked with over two thousand clients since starting his speaking business. Simon T. Bailey International, his company, has multiple verticals, each with a different clientele, including:

- Prospective clients who want to hire Simon for a keynote speech for the first time.
- Returning clients who have previously hired Simon for a keynote speech.
- Members of BrilliantU, Simon's online membership community with courses and live sessions.
- Individuals who want to apply to Simon's Brilliant Coaching program, where he matches up accepted individuals with a Simon-approved leadership and development coach.

- Readers who have purchased one of Simon's many books.
- Social media followers who could convert into a BrilliantU member someday.

Looking at Simon's accomplishments, you might think he has a team of thirty people or more. But Simon has a nimble and competent team of three people. Like many small business owners, it's important to Simon that clients have a personalized and high-quality experience, so he's kept his team small intentionally.

I'm sure you can imagine the possible opportunities for artificial intelligence to play a role on Simon's team. By implementing AI tools, particularly on the customer service side of things, Simon could give his customers a faster and more personalized experience—even more than if he grew his team. Here's a breakdown of the main opportunities:

- **Consolidating data on multiple business verticals:** With the wide variety of business verticals, Simon appeals to a diverse range of customers. With books around $15 and speaking engagements well into five figures, his prospective and current clientele have very different needs and expectations. Artificial intelligence can merge Simon's business vertical data to create proper customer segments, which then inform the experience that customers receive whenever they have a query.
- **Personalizing speaking engagement clients:** With a speaking engagement every three to four days, there is ample communication from and with speaking engagement clients related to the work, preparation, travel, bulk book deals, technical requirements, and more. AI tools can help streamline repeat questions and escalate to a human representative when necessary.
- **Engaging on social media:** Instagram, LinkedIn, and TikTok are important vehicles for nurturing current and future BrilliantU members. Employing an artificial intelligence chatbot could help streamline frequently asked questions from members quickly, ensuring people feel heard and receive a quick resolution.

- **Providing support to BrilliantU members:** Simon's BrilliantU membership community thrives through a video library and daily discussion board on a platform I use myself called Uscreen. Outside of the private interface, members often email questions about their membership status, the next live call dates, and what courses to take, and an artificial intelligence tool could help maintain membership satisfaction and overall retention.
- **Managing Brilliant Coaching clients:** Many of Simon's keynote attendees are managers, directors, and executives who want to improve their leadership skills. Simon's Brilliant Coaching program receives frequent correspondence from potential and current members—either wanting more information about the service or wanting to touch base between sessions with their coach. Artificial intelligence could cater its answers based on where the customer is in their journey.

Steps to Integrate AI for Customer Service

Let's go through the steps Simon can take to implement AI into his workflow. My hope is this example will be a source of inspiration for your own business. Any kind of technological change can be intimidating, but through these simple stages, Simon can gradually integrate AI solutions, starting with identifying his goals and business needs.

1. **Figure out goals and needs:** First, Simon and his team must determine their key needs and goals. From my standpoint, this would include:
   - Streamlining communications across past and present speaking clients, book buyers, members, and coaches.
   - Creating efficiencies and automations to free up Simon and his team.
   - Consolidating data to create customer profiles.
   - Measuring volume across interactions to scale and staff the necessary customer service support.

2. **Determine tool(s):** Next, they'd want to determine the best tools for their needs. Simon and his team could review the tool suggestions in this book and discuss them with a generative AI tool. They may consider trying a prompt like this (which you can modify and try too).

AI in Action

Try a variation of this prompt:

 I'm Simon T. Bailey, a motivational speaker with a multifaceted business operation. My team is small, but we manage a significant workload across different verticals. Annually, I do about one hundred speaking engagements for large companies and conferences, which require personalized coordination and extensive communication, including travel arrangements and customizing keynotes to client needs.

Additionally, I run BrilliantU, an online membership community offering courses, live sessions, and more. I've authored multiple books and offer a coaching service connecting clients with a team of coaches who follow my leadership approach.

Our customer interactions span various platforms: direct texts, social media (TikTok, Instagram, Facebook, LinkedIn), and our main website hosted on Squarespace. Given these dynamics, I'm seeking an AI-driven customer service solution that is cost effective and can efficiently manage inquiries and support across these channels. The tool should ideally support automated responses and ticket triage, and it should integrate well with Squarespace for live chat functionalities.

Given our small team and the volume of our engagements, it's crucial to have a system that can also provide insights into customer service performance and help manage the workload. I'm looking for recommendations for a one-stop-shop AI tool that can cater to these needs without breaking the bank, as options like HubSpot are out of our budget range. Can you please make a suggestion?

 Given the specifics of your business, Simon, and your preferences for a cost-effective AI tool that can cater to various aspects of customer service, including handling texts and integrating with your Squarespace website, I recommend considering Freshdesk as a versatile, all-in-one solution. Freshdesk is not only more budget friendly compared to HubSpot; it also offers a comprehensive suite of features that can support your diverse business needs, from managing speaking engagements to handling inquiries for BrilliantU and your coaching services. Here's why Freshdesk stands out as a suitable choice for you:

1. **Omnichannel Support:** Freshdesk enables seamless management of customer communications across multiple channels, including email, social media, chat, and, importantly for your needs, SMS for text messages. This ensures you can stay connected with your clients and audience wherever they prefer to reach out.

2. **Squarespace Integration:** Integrating Freshdesk with your Squarespace website is straightforward. You can also easily add the Freshchat chat widget to your site, allowing real-time interactions with website visitors. This feature can help engage potential clients for speaking engagements and users interested in your membership program or coaching services.

3. **AI-Powered Chatbots and Automation:** Freshdesk's AI assistant, Freddy, offers automated service capabilities such as answering FAQs, ticket routing, and even gathering preliminary information from clients about their event requirements or coaching inquiries. This can significantly reduce the manual workload on your small team.

4. **Cost-Effectiveness:** Freshdesk provides a flexible pricing model with various tiers, including a free tier with basic features and more advanced tiers that are competitively priced. This allows you to choose a plan that fits your budget while still accessing powerful AI tools to enhance your customer service.

5. **Scalability:** As your speaking engagements grow and your BrilliantU community expands, Freshdesk can scale with your business. You can add more advanced features or increase your agent count within the platform without needing to switch to a different service provider.

6. **Reporting and Analytics:** Freshdesk offers comprehensive analytics and reporting tools that give you insights into customer satisfaction, agent performance, and common inquiry trends. These insights can inform business decisions, helping you refine your offerings and improve client and customer experiences.

Here's how you would implement Freshdesk for your business:

- **Start with a Plan:** Begin with Freshdesk's free plan or a lower-tier paid plan to evaluate its fit for your business. You can upgrade as your needs grow.

- **Customize Your Setup:** Use Freshdesk to set up dedicated support channels for each of your business verticals (speaking engagements, BrilliantU, coaching services, etc.), ensuring inquiries are efficiently organized and managed.

- **Leverage Freddy AI:** Activate Freddy AI for automated responses and support on your Squarespace site and SMS communications, ensuring that common questions are immediately addressed.

By opting for Freshdesk, you'll have access to a cost-effective, comprehensive AI tool that meets your diverse business needs, supports your growth, and enhances the quality of your customer service—all without stretching your budget.

In this instance, the generative AI is right—Freshdesk is a great solution for Simon's business needs. It has automated ticket routing, canned responses, knowledge base development, and analytics, and it can also be customized to integrate with Simon's existing software. Freshdesk creates and updates detailed customer profiles that consider information from interactions across multiple platforms, and it also consolidates customers' purchasing history, previous customer service queries, and other data. The tool also permits human agents to add custom tags and notes to customer profiles, so Simon's team could make notes of his relationship with clients outside of what Freshdesk has observed.

Simon's website is the main hub of his business. It houses all of his keynote programs, book links, membership community information, and more. A chatbot will save Simon and his team ample time on basic inquiries and questions from clients. Excitingly for Simon, Freshdesk's Freddy AI is a chatbot that easily integrates with Squarespace. It can answer FAQs, provide detailed product questions, capture information from visitors for his sales team (or sales AI) to follow up with, and, best of all, provide completely personalized interactions based on the user's past and present behavior.

1. **Integrate and configure:** Now that Simon has selected Freshdesk, it's time to begin integrating. With Freshdesk, Simon's team will be prompted to go through the following actions:

   - Set up the account by choosing a plan that best fits Simon's business needs.
   - Insert operational details, like business hours, the necessary fields for capturing ticket information, and the ticket statuses that would be most helpful to Simon and his team.
   - Import data (if applicable) through the platform's innate tools, such as adding existing customer inquiries, uploading current client details, and creating specific customer profiles (note: this part might require some manual effort at first, so I recommend setting aside some regular team meetings to review this data together).
   - Integrate the email addresses of each client and customer-facing team member within Simon's company, including Simon himself (Freshdesk's technology will automatically create customer service tickets based on the nature of the email).
   - Set up automation workflows so Freshdesk can learn how to prioritize and escalate different support tickets based on the sender's status and the keywords used in the query.
   - Turn on Freddy AI, Freshdesk's AI tool, so it can use machine learning and natural language processing to learn Simon's most common inquiries in its initial learning phase.
   - Add in all other customer support channels, like Simon's social media channels, and also add Freddy AI to Simon's website, which ensures a consistent message (from Freshdesk) at every customer touchpoint.
   - Practice using the new system and have a team touch base every week to review Freshdesk's results, making any changes as necessary.

2. **Communicate, monitor, and adjust:** The toughest part of new systems is enforcing the change instead of slipping into old habits. It could be worth sending out a communication to past and current customers about the latest systems for support tickets. (Be sure to list the many benefits, such as instantaneous feedback and rapid escalation to human representatives!) Continue to touch base with your team to get their thoughts on the systems; if you need to make adjustments, adjust quickly. Also, make a habit of frequently reviewing customer service reporting. Consider running a monthly report (or having a team member run a monthly report) and ask the following questions:

   - What's going well in our new customer service setup?
   - What percentage or volume of inquiries is our AI currently handling?
   - What are the top three topics or queries most handled by our AI?
   - Has the AI reduced response wait times?
   - How often does the AI need to escalate to a human agent?
   - What are the top three topics or queries most handled by our human agents after escalation?
   - Are there any technical issues we've encountered with the AI?
   - What three changes can we implement next week to create more efficiencies?

PRIVACY, CUSTOMER SERVICE, AND AI

Like many people in leadership roles within businesses, you may be concerned about having AI as the first "line of defense" with customer interactions. For artificial intelligence to be involved with customer service, the technology will have access to private information about your company and clientele. While it is exciting how artificial intelligence can help businesses, privacy and security are real and valid concerns.

Let's face it: Giving artificial intelligence access to your business data can be nerve-racking, especially since this technology is relatively new in this application. Your customers' data is invaluable; any mishandling could potentially erode trust and, worse, permanently lose a customer. Let's explore some common (and completely understandable) anxieties with AI and your customers' data.

Data Breaches

In this technological age, data breaches apply to all businesses with any online element—not just artificial intelligence technology. To protect your business against hacks, you'll want to follow basic security to keep your customer and business information safe. Use strong passwords across your company (ideally using a password manager with an authenticator) to keep data across all verticals accessible to designated people. Consider hiring a cybersecurity expert to regularly test your systems for weaknesses that hackers might exploit and be sure to mention your new artificial intelligence workflows.

Following Data Compliance

Staying in line with the most current data regulations is critical for your business and your customers' safety. Legal penalties for noncompliance with data protection and privacy laws can be hefty, and that doesn't consider the additional costs of reputational damage. To follow the latest data rules, ensure you are up-to-date with customer privacy laws and, importantly, ensure your business complies with those laws. (You can use the research skills of generative AI to help you with this monthly or quarterly.) When employing AI tools, choose tools committed to protection and data privacy through features like anonymization abilities and data encryption. I also recommend checking that your tool holds certifications or statements demonstrating a commitment to modern security standards, like compliance with the California Consumer Privacy Act (CCPA) or the General Data Protection Regulation (GDPR).

Managing Data Rights

If you're in a B2C company (and even, in many cases, a B2B company), then you recognize that customers are the lifeblood of your business. Transparency about your data and security practices is essential to develop and sustain trust. Ensure that your privacy policies are comprehensive and written out so your customers know exactly how their data is collected, used, and stored, particularly regarding artificial intelligence. It's also recommended that your privacy policy is easily accessible in the footer of your website; these simple open gestures demonstrate that your business prioritizes your customers' data privacy, and in some instances, it may be required by law. Customers have the right to consent to their data use, so it could be worth obtaining explicit consent about using AI for customer data when registering for an account or contacting customer service.

Lastly, since transparency is the unofficial theme of this section, in the event of a data breach, notify your customers once an issue has been identified and resolved. Include the incident's scope and (if you can) the data affected, along with any other steps customers can take to protect themselves.

FINAL THOUGHTS ABOUT AI AND CUSTOMER SERVICE

As you can see, there is no shortage of customer service tools to help your business. If you're ever overwhelmed by the possibilities, pick one tool and give it a go. You don't have to implement every tool you try, and you'll learn quickly if a tool is a good fit for your business needs.

My friend Kris Kashtanova, an AI artist, shared a unique and inspiring perspective on social media: "Artificial intelligence technology presents a great time to develop workflows that amplify human creativity and look deep into how we can use AI for good." I couldn't have said it better.

Here's what is exciting about artificial intelligence's future role in customer service: It presents an opportunity to meet and exceed customer expectations. You'll address core concerns faster through AI responses and a developed knowledge base. If an issue requires a human agent, the customer will be greeted by a focused representative who isn't burdened by the stress of unprioritized and repetitive tasks. This journey will be ongoing, so stay committed to fine-tuning your AI processes to make it work for you.

AI + Finance and Accounting

There's no way around it: Successful businesses understand their financials. If you understand cash flow, budgeting, costs, market conditions, and risk management, you can make important decisions to help your business grow confidently. Whether you have an internal finance team or trust an external expert, financial literacy is paramount for leaders in any organization.

Artificial intelligence's data capacity and analysis, machine-learning abilities, and overall natural language processing are game changers for small business owners who want to streamline and improve their financials. Artificial intelligence's machine learning defies human bias, creating objective analyses and predictions based on history and helping businesses make the right decisions quickly. Businesses can also leverage AI's natural language processing to understand financial analyses clearly, and artificial intelligence can break down complex observations into terms you can understand. Combine all this with AI's specialties of automating repetitive tasks, and you've just leveled up your business's financials.

ARTIFICIAL INTELLIGENCE: WHERE SILICON VALLEY MEETS WALL STREET

The traditional finance world involves humans scouring financial data to uncover the meaning behind market data, economic indicators, financial statements, and more. As we've seen in other industries, artificial intelligence is a transformative force bringing immense data processing capabilities and analyses that are better and faster than human brains. Simply put, artificial intelligence technology can remove errors, working hours, and the risk of brain fatigue from financial analysis and decision-making. With artificial intelligence rapidly processing complex financial and economic data, workers do not need to pore over spreadsheets and data points. Instead of making sense of data, businesses can focus on taking action from data.

In traditional finance, bigger companies were at an advantage, where more brains meant more data interpretation. Now, with artificial intelligence, the playing field is leveled. You don't need to be a large corporation with a big financial department to make informed financial decisions, predict market moves, or process large amounts of data. Thanks to artificial intelligence's many financial tools, one-person businesses can leverage sophisticated analyses to make sound, data-rooted choices—for their businesses, departments, and clients.

Small businesses can also generate the financial efficiencies previously experienced by large companies through artificial intelligence. Instead of hiring a financial team for routine tasks like bookkeeping, invoicing, and payroll, small businesses can save on costs while improving the final output by automating these processes through artificial intelligence. Instead of paying for labor costs to manage your business's finances manually, you can utilize those funds toward strategic minds who can grow or improve your business.

AI CAN HELP YOU MANAGE YOUR CASH FLOW

No matter what type of business you have, insight about cash flow can be critical for success. To grow a business, you need to invest time, people, technology, advertising, office space, supplies, and the list goes on—and cash flow analysis is the only way to know what you can afford. Regularly conducting cash flow analysis will ensure you don't commit to more than you can afford. Your solvency will also impact your operations, ensuring you can continue to cover operational costs in the face of unexpected or temporary setbacks.

Your cash flow cycles can also tell you the best moments to make investments—in the short and long term. This might mean expanding to a new warehouse, building a new product, or adding an executive to your team. Visibility into your cash flow will empower you to know if and *when* you can make those critical investments. On the flip side of investing in your business, you can also pinpoint areas to reduce spending and, ultimately, save money.

Being on top of your cash flow is critical for overall financial management beyond general operation. If you ever want to seek investor funding, secure a loan, or even sell your business, that lender or investor will want visibility into your cash flow. To put it bluntly, understanding where your money is coming and going can be the backbone of any informed decision-making—and artificial intelligence can tell you with specificity and precision.

Cash Flow Pre-AI

Most businesses today rely on basic accounting software (or even manual tracking) to understand what cash is coming in and out. Between expenses, payroll, late customer payments, rent, and all the other transactions that come with business, these numerous calculations require immense effort and time to manage. Management can be contaminated by human error, where one mislabeled item or one wrong calculation can impact an entire month's reporting. With this type of manual tracking, reactive decision-making is inevitable. Instead of being conscientious of cash flow issues that could occur in the future, you only react to issues in real time, adding stress and commanding resources that could otherwise go toward planning or business operations.

Before artificial intelligence, businesses would have blinders on when looking at market conditions. They'd make predictions on market trends and external factors from limited data points, and then, by the time their human workers sifted through and analyzed data, they risked being outdated.

AI Cash Flow in Action

Artificial intelligence makes complex analysis readily available for businesses of all sizes. Whether you're looking for assistance with forecasting, an objective eye on predictions and trends in your industry, or even just help with bookkeeping, artificial intelligence can do it all—and often for a reasonable price. Let's dig into some specific examples of artificial intelligence in action.

PREFERRED PLATFORMS FOR ACCOUNTING AND CASH FLOW

A wide range of financial tools are available, some with limited capabilities and some with more complex multifunctional capabilities. Here are some you should test out for your small business:

- **FlyFin.** FlyFin utilizes AI technology to simplify the tax filing process for freelancers and small business owners. FlyFin's AI algorithm integrates with financial accounts and scans transactions to uncover potential tax deductions, ensuring users don't miss out on savings. It addresses essential tax queries such as "How can I maximize my deductions?" and "What are the tax implications of a new expense?" FlyFin offers features like real-time deduction tracking and automatic expense categorization, eliminating the manual effort typically associated with tax preparation. The platform provides a detailed, constantly updated overview of your tax situation, streamlining personal and business tax management through its AI-driven insights.
- **Rossum.** Rossum provides AI solutions for handling documents, including an automated system for managing accounts payable. This system adapts to different document layouts using advanced AI, includes tools to track its efficiency, and integrates easily with existing accounts payable systems. Additionally, it offers customization options through extensions and a user-friendly platform that requires minimal coding.
- **PlanGuru.** PlanGuru can generate financial analyses within minutes by importing your historical results into its platform. The tool also creates income statements, balance sheets, and cash flow

statements, giving businesses a launching pad for AI-driven projections up to ten years in the future. It's worth noting that PlanGuru's software can also work for nonprofit organizations, and it can help with workforce planning, issuing lines of credit, and more.

- **Quadient Accounts Receivable.** With Quadient Accounts Receivable, your entire accounts receivable process can be automated. Formerly known as YayPay, the tool touts its ability to help you collect cash 34% faster with three times less work through automation. In addition to sending and following up on invoices, Quadient Accounts Receivable uses AI-driven predictive analytics to forecast payment dates down to the individual customer. This way, you can have highly accurate cash flow predictions, allowing you to plan accordingly.

- **Xero.** This AI-driven tool helps small businesses send invoices, manage expenses, create and pay bills, control their budget, and even access credit to grow. The tool integrates intelligent features like automated bank reconciliation, data capture, international payments management, and cash flow forecasting. Syncing with multiple major accounting software, this tool makes it easy to see your business cash flow activities, including proofs of payment and other supporting documents. Its budget management solutions allow for different employee access levels, protecting you from surprise expenses.

- **HoneyBook.** HoneyBook is designed to streamline client management for small businesses and freelancers. Using AI, HoneyBook automates administrative tasks such as contract creation, invoice generation, and payment tracking. The platform integrates with your calendar to schedule meetings and send reminders, ensuring you stay on top of your client interactions. HoneyBook's AI also provides insights into your project pipeline, helping you manage workload and forecast future business needs effectively.

- **Expensify.** Expensify brings ease to managing paper receipts through its user-friendly mobile app that employs SmartScan technology to extract invoice and receipt details to categorize and match transactions automatically. The software also has AI-powered auditing technology, which ensures correct exchange rates, confirms transaction accuracy, and detects duplicate entries, giving you the most accurate insights into your company's finances.

- **Rydoo.** Rydoo's smart AI technology handles expense management for small businesses. Through the Rydoo app, you and your team can take photos of any driven miles and expenses. Then, the AI will automatically cross-reference detailed information to corporate card transaction records. The tool connects with over thirty-five other travel, HR, finance, and ERP (enterprise resource planning) software, allowing you to have fully integrated data. The tool enables you to implement company policies (like spending limits and allowable expenses), and its AI will flag any that don't comply. Its artificial intelligence can also use predictive analytics to forecast future expenses and suggest areas to cut spending.

- **MileIQ.** MileIQ is a mileage tracking app that leverages AI to automatically log and categorize your drives. By learning your driving habits, MileIQ can differentiate between business and personal trips (by swiping right or left), providing you with accurate mileage reports for tax deductions and expense reimbursements. The app syncs seamlessly with accounting software, making it easy to integrate your mileage data into your financial records.

- **TurnKey Lender.** With AI-driven credit scoring, TurnKey Lender evaluates multiple data sources to assess your customers' credit risk. The software considers the unique needs of your specific business model, helping you devise a fully automated process for consumer lending, such as personal loans, payday loans, leasing, medical credit, and more. On the commercial lending front, the tool's analysis model applies a score and decision to every potential customer, along with document management, reporting, and built-in compliance.

- **Sage Intacct.** Sage Intacct's software gives you ample visibility into your business's financials through account receivable processes, general ledger functions, cash management reporting, order management, and more. With over seventeen thousand customers, the tool consolidates across datasets to give you real-time insights through multidimensional reporting. Its AI uses machine learning to identify anomalies, trends, and errors that could lead to financial impact. It also streamlines processes that are prone to auditing, such as transaction recording, revenue recognition, and compliance, ensuring your business is aligned with financial regulations.

- **QuickBooks.** You might be surprised to see QuickBooks on here, but the enterprise does use AI! The software uses artificial intelligence in multiple ways, including automated bookkeeping, receipt capture, and anomaly detection. Its artificial intelligence applies machine learning to analyze historical data, report about your business's projected cash flow, and suggest ways to optimize expenses, tax deductions, and other important financial considerations.

Forecast Cash Flow Through Predictive Analytics

What AI can do: Analyze historical sales data and external information (like local events and economic trends) to predict changes in cash flow.

Recommended AI tools for this task: Xero, QuickBooks, PlanGuru

Data you might need on hand: Historical sales data, economic trends data, seasonal sales patterns, inventory levels, marketing campaign schedules

Let's imagine you're a bakery owner in San Francisco. An AI tool could analyze your historical sales data, upcoming events in your neighborhood, and other local economic trends. Through its machine-learning algorithms, artificial intelligence might anticipate a major increase in cash flow over the holiday season, where its system identifies patterns within and outside your business. When the AI arrives at this prediction, you as the bakery owner would receive a notification and recommendations on maximizing this opportunity, such as increasing operating hours, hiring more staff, and increasing inventory levels.

If you were, say, a leader at a manufacturing plant in Detroit, artificial intelligence could be particularly helpful in cash flow and inventory management. If AI were to analyze relevant data patterns, it could anticipate an order slowdown from a major automotive parts manufacturer client due to external factors such as economic downturns. From there, artificial intelligence might recommend strategies for the anticipated cash flow dip, like refraining from unnecessary expenses, negotiating with other suppliers, and using other tactics to preserve cash.

In both scenarios, the businesses are at the mercy of external economics, but with artificial intelligence as a proactive advisor, they can adjust their plans accordingly. Depending on the artificial intelligence tool, the notifications and AI involvements can greatly vary in detail, but even a minor notification from artificial intelligence could supply business owners with critical data that would otherwise be missed.

Automate Invoices

What AI can do: Create and distribute invoices, match invoices with purchase orders, and follow up when invoices are due.

Recommended AI tools for this task: Xero, QuickBooks, HoneyBook, Zoho Books, FreshBooks

Data you might need on hand: Customer contact information, purchase order details, payment terms, service or product descriptions, time-tracking data (for service-based businesses)

Sending manual invoices is a thing of the past now that AI is available to small businesses. There are ample tools on the market that harness artificial intelligence technology to create and distribute invoices, pair invoices with purchase orders, and follow up when invoices are due. Instead of worrying about invoicing coming to a halt when the responsible employee is on vacation, you can trust artificial intelligence to automate the entire process. Beyond managing invoice operations, AI goes a step further, giving you insights into cash flow based on invoice activities.

If you're a service-based company, like a digital marketing agency, you'll benefit from AI's automatic scheduling and management of client invoices. Instead of manually calculating your team's hours on a project, artificial intelligence can integrate with your project management software and time-tracking tools to create an invoice based on working time. You can also program the AI to your agency policies to ensure a client's invoice complies with your agreements. As an example, if a digital marketing agency operating in New York City's working hours on a $3,000 project ended up going over budget to $3,750, a few things could happen:

- The agency could program the artificial intelligence to notify the project manager when the team has hit or exceeded the budget, allowing for a conversation with the client before any surprise invoices are created.
- The agency could set up an approval workflow for invoice generation with the AI, where an invoice beyond the agreed scope needs to get approval from the account director before being distributed to the client.
- The agency could require the AI to provide a detailed breakdown of all working hours, along with a summary of other factors that caused the project to go over budget when creating and sending an invoice.
- The agency could proactively teach the AI to alert the team if a project is veering over budget (before it does) by analyzing past logged time.

Analyze Expenses in Real Time

What AI can do: Monitor expenses across every department regardless of software and make recommendations based on data received.

Recommended AI tools for this task: Expensify, MileIQ, Rydoo

Data you might need on hand: Expense receipts, bank statements, credit card transactions, mileage data

Before artificial intelligence, companies would have to manually track and categorize all expenses. With human minds processing and analyzing, logging expenses can take weeks (or even months!), with information scattered across paper receipts, spreadsheets, and bank statements. Once an accountant or controller gets access to the expense reports, they only get a picture of what happened in the past, with no insight into how these patterns translate to the future.

Artificial intelligence technology can guide small businesses in managing their expenses right *now*. An example of this could be with a tech start-up in Silicon Valley. The start-up is growing rapidly after receiving a Series B investment, and there are multiple departments, each with its subscriptions and expenses. If this company incorporated an AI-powered financial management tool, employees' expenses across departments could be monitored and analyzed in real time. If two departments (like marketing and sales) used different tools for email marketing, artificial intelligence could flag these conflicting platforms and identify an opportunity to negotiate a bulk discount by merging under one subscription. Or the AI could notice low use in a particular subscription among workers, highlighting an opportunity to cancel the subscription. These types of flags might not be noticed by humans immersed in a company's day-to-day operations; it's with AI's insights that this tech company could free up capital.

For a business in the hospitality industry, artificial intelligence can monitor fluctuating operating expenses, like utilities, and make recommendations. Take a boutique hotel chain in Miami, which has peak tourism seasons leading to increased electricity and air conditioning usage. AI could monitor, analyze, and flag utility usage across multiple properties to pinpoint inefficiencies and usage patterns. Once the AI notices a trend, it could alert about the cost-saving opportunity. For example, if there's a midday spike because of inefficient HVAC systems, the hotel might be inclined to install smart thermostats or upgrade to an energy-efficient system. The AI might notice a steady increase in water usage that's in fact a leak, which could kick-start repairs before the situation gets out of hand.

Both scenarios involve ways that AI can help you run your business smarter. While artificial intelligence quietly runs in the background, you can instead focus on managing and growing your small business and be assured that AI will notify you about any issue or opportunity well in advance.

Assess Credit Risk

What AI can do: Analyze a customer's risk level and recommend credit terms.

Recommended AI tools for this task: TurnKey Lender

Data you might need on hand: Customer credit history, financial statements, payment history, industry trends

If your business provides payment plans or delayed payments, you're actually in the business of lending. At its simplest level, by deferring accounts receivable, you essentially loan your customers money—your business's money. In the old days, the main ways you'd evaluate a customer were through credit scores and financial statements. These two measurements indicate part of a company's financial health but certainly not the full picture.

Now, with artificial intelligence, you do indeed get the full picture of someone's credit risk. AI's advanced data processing capabilities can unveil a client with mass potential while indicating when a client, even with a good credit score, could be risky. Some of the credit risk data points that artificial intelligence measures include:

- Industry trends, particularly concerning the customer.
- Overall social media sentiment, indicating customer satisfaction.
- Potential future financial behavior based on past actions.

Beyond evaluation, artificial intelligence can help you devise wholly customized credit terms to suit that customer. You'll be poised to make a sale while minimizing your company's exposure to risk. The AI can provide you with this insight in real time, ensuring market conditions are considered right until you offer your deal.

Suppose an agricultural cooperative in Iowa uses AI technology to assess credit risk. The company could evaluate farmers on a case-by-case basis through artificial intelligence technology. If a farmer requested seeds on credit, the cooperative could use artificial intelligence to assess past crop yields and market conditions to predict future crop yields. Through artificial intelligence, the organization could ensure any credited farms have a strong likelihood of repaying, thereby protecting their cash flow and reducing risk for the high volatility and seasonality of farming. The artificial intelligence would also uncover farmers who are highly poised for solid repayments, even if their financial statements are dicey.

Artificial intelligence can support your credit risk assessments well past the initial inquiry. Beyond extending the credit and setting the credit terms with dynamic pricing for each customer, AI tools can continuously monitor your customers' financial health by analyzing payment patterns and market conditions throughout the course of your arrangement. If artificial intelligence flags a drop in financial health, the credit terms could be adjusted in real time, helping to protect your business proactively.

One thing to mention here: Artificial intelligence in credit assessments and lending is at its best when combined with a human touch. Whether managing a store credit card program, offering trade credit, generating payment plans, or issuing lines of credit, AI's beauty lies in its ability to help you say yes to more customers—assuming they're low-risk for your company—so you can forge and deepen business relationships.

Manage Your Budget

What AI can do: Proactively track your company's financial health by analyzing financial data.

Recommended AI tools for this task: QuickBooks, Xero, HoneyBook, PlanGuru

Data you might need on hand: Income statements, expense reports, projected revenue, cash flow statements

Thanks to artificial intelligence, you and your team no longer have to pore over receipts, spreadsheets, and invoices to understand your company's finances. Whether you have a few daily expenses or thousands, AI gets you out of the weeds and into your corner office by giving you a reliable, efficient, and timely look into your business's financial health. Artificial intelligence bridges financial data and strategic decision-making, helping you devote more energy to decisions that move you forward without posing financial risks. From managing budgets to anticipating cash flow lapses, AI is a Swiss Army knife of proactive financial management.

AI in Practice

To demonstrate artificial intelligence's incredible abilities with budget management, I want to use my longtime client Custom Design & Construction (CD&C) as an example. Founded in 1988 and possessing a stellar reputation from hundreds of clients, CD&C is a design-build firm based in El Segundo, California. They handle remodeling for clients from initial architectural design to construction to final interior design. While many firms in the remodeling industry focus on just one element (like construction), CD&C is the primary point of contact on client projects from start to finish, meaning budget management is paramount for their clients and, in turn, CD&C's small business.

While CD&C is a small business, its work is extensive, and its team is efficient. With about ten employees and a team of trusted contractors, they could use artificial intelligence in their workflow to understand their finances from a macro and micro level. By implementing AI, they could:

- Improve their project management budgeting process, with alerts if they're ever nearing or exceeding budgets.
- Automate their financial operations, including invoice and expense tracking.
- Forecast cash flow to prepare for potential market trends.
- Plan for various scenarios like hiring new staff members or taking on new projects.

- Prepare for the future and have advanced time for strategic decision-making.
- Improve their outreach efforts based on cash flow projections.

In summary, incorporating artificial intelligence would help the CD&C team save time on manual financial efforts and put their team's minds toward more fruitful endeavors. Let's discover how.

Finding the Right Tools for Your Systems

Before integrating artificial intelligence into your workflow, it's important to freely converse with generative AI to understand the tool combination that best suits your needs. Every AI tool has its strengths, some overlapping, and I firmly believe in adopting as few tools as possible initially, knowing you can always add more later.

Here's an example of how CD&C could get tool recommendations for their unique situation using a generative AI tool such as ChatGPT.

AI in Action

Try a variation of this prompt:

 Hi, I am Beth from Custom Design & Construction, a design-build firm based in El Segundo, California. We are a small business with about ten employees and a team of trusted contractors. We do home remodeling of all sizes. We want to use AI to automate our finances, manage client budgets, and also make predictions about cash flow so we have better insights into the company. We currently use QuickBooks and Buildertrend. We want to use as few tools as possible. What do you recommend we use and why?

It's great to hear that you're looking to leverage AI to streamline your operations at Custom Design & Construction. Given your current use of QuickBooks and Buildertrend, along with your desire to automate finances, manage client budgets effectively, and predict cash flow for better company insights, I recommend enhancing your tool kit with QuickBooks Online Advanced, Buildertrend, and introducing Float. Here's why these three tools are a strong fit for your needs:

QuickBooks Online Advanced:

- **Automated Financial Management:** QuickBooks Online Advanced offers advanced features over the basic version, such as more comprehensive automation for invoicing, expense tracking, and financial reporting. This level of automation can significantly reduce manual data entry and increase accuracy in your financial records.

- **Enhanced Reporting and Insights:** With QuickBooks Online Advanced, you gain access to more detailed reporting and analytics tools. These can provide deeper insights into your financial health, helping you make informed decisions about your business.

Buildertrend:

- **Project Management and Budgeting:** As you're already using Buildertrend, you know its strengths in project management. Leveraging its full capabilities for budget tracking and client communication ensures that you can keep each remodeling project on track and within budget. It also streamlines communication with your team and clients, keeping everyone updated on project progress.

• **Integration with QuickBooks:** The seamless integration between Buildertrend and QuickBooks (including Online Advanced) means that financial data flows directly between your project management and accounting systems. This integration ensures that you have a holistic view of each project's financial health and overall business performance.

Float:

- **Cash Flow Forecasting:** Float is a powerful cash flow forecasting tool that integrates with the online version of QuickBooks. It uses AI to analyze your historical financial data to predict future cash flow scenarios, which is invaluable for a business like yours where cash flow can be significantly impacted by project timelines and payment milestones.

- **Scenario Planning:** Float allows you to create and compare different financial scenarios, such as taking on new projects or changes in payment terms. This feature can help you plan for various futures, ensuring that you're prepared for any financial situation.

Why These Three?

- **Comprehensive Solution with Minimal Overlap:** Together, QuickBooks Online Advanced, Buildertrend, and Float cover a wide range of your AI and automation needs without significant overlap in functionality. This setup ensures you're not paying for redundant features.

- **Streamlined Operations:** This combination minimizes the number of tools you need to manage, streamlining your operations. It allows you to focus more on your core business of designing and building, rather than managing multiple software solutions.

- **Better Decision-Making:** With accurate financial data, project management insights, and cash flow predictions, you're equipped to make informed decisions about your business's future. This could range from taking on new projects, managing staffing levels, or adjusting project timelines to ensure financial stability.

- **Future-Proofing Your Business:** The AI-driven insights and forecasting capabilities provided by these tools can help you anticipate and navigate the challenges that come with running a small business, especially in the dynamic field of home remodeling.

Beth, by using QuickBooks Online Advanced for comprehensive financial management, Buildertrend for project management and client budgeting, and Float for cash flow forecasting and scenario planning, Custom Design & Construction will be well positioned to manage and grow as a business efficiently and effectively. These tools will provide the automation and insights needed to stay ahead in the competitive design-build industry.

The key part of this interaction is Beth listing the software that CD&C already uses. Like solving a puzzle, generative AI can determine what tools best integrate with the systems you already have in place, making the adoption even more natural. Lucky for Beth, two of the tools they use already have artificial intelligence capabilities—unbeknownst to them—making the integration even easier than anticipated.

Implementing Budgeting Tools

Since CD&C is already using QuickBooks and Buildertrend, their first course of action will be to familiarize themselves with the capabilities of each tool. In my experience, many of us already have subscriptions in our business, but with looming to-do lists and unexpected fires, taking the time to understand and utilize all of a subscription's features can get put on the back burner. So, it would be beneficial for Beth to appoint a half day of work to dedicate to learning each tool. Alternatively, she could appoint a team member to each tool (QuickBooks and Buildertrend) and have them determine how they could be used for CD&C's needs.

After the research day is done, CD&C would ideally have a bulleted list of what automation and functions would take place in each tool, like this:

QuickBooks
- Housing all financial transactions (like invoices, expenses, and payments).
- Invoicing all clients and managing accounts receivable.
- Tracking (note: not loading) expenses across the team and projects.
- Managing employee payroll, including salary, taxes, and deductions.
- Organizing financial information for tax preparation through their artificial intelligence's automatic categorization.

Buildertrend
- Automatically loading all client leads via Zapier integration.
- Tracking sales pipeline by client status, source, and potential project value.
- Creating and distributing proposals to clients.
- Housing all client interaction records, including emails, calls, and meeting notes.
- Loading in any project-specific expenses.
- Monitoring client project budgets in real time.
- Tracking time of employees and contracts on different projects.
- Sharing documents and photos with clients.

I should note that there are some overlaps between QuickBooks Online Advanced's and Buildertrend's functionalities, and in this list, I chose what tool was most appropriate for that particular feature. As an example, both QuickBooks and Buildertrend offer expense tracking. I made the decision to have employees load in their expenses to Buildertrend for a few reasons:

- The employee can note what project the expense is for, so the client's budget includes it.
- Buildertrend syncs with QuickBooks, so the expense will still load in QuickBooks.
- The majority of team members will now only need one login (Buildertrend).

So, you can see how Buildertrend will be the app predominantly used by team members and clients, and then select management or owners like Beth can get access to QuickBooks. Buildertrend is essentially for work that's *for* the business, whereas QuickBooks can be used for work that's *on* the business.

Now that CD&C is clear on what existing tools do what, they're ready to add on Float. After purchasing a Float subscription, Beth can integrate Float directly with QuickBooks, so the AI tools have a clear picture of past and current financial activity. As cash comes in, Float can provide a financial forecast that updates to the minute, helping Beth plan for the future.

Float can also help Beth understand, from a high level, how projects impact CD&C's overall finances. By analyzing cash coming in and out of the business, Float can set the stage for detailed project cost analysis, goal setting for income benchmarks, and modeling various scenarios. Beth will be poised to make better decisions about CD&C, like what projects are worth pursuing and if she needs to hire more team members, all through the power of artificial intelligence and automation.

Oversee Assets, Investments, and Tax Compliance

What AI can do: Assist with big-picture financial management tasks.

Recommended AI tools for this task: Asset Panda, Wealthfront, QuickBooks, TurboTax, H&R Block, Xero, Zoho Books, FlyFin, Avalara, Wave Accounting

Data you might need on hand: Asset inventory, investment portfolios, tax documents, financial statements, compliance records, expense reports

Small businesses that leverage artificial intelligence benefit from the technology's ability to fit into nearly any organizational need. In addition to the day-to-day business minutia, AI can also be used for a much larger scope, particularly in financial management.

Asset Management

If you have physical, technological, or even intangible assets, artificial intelligence can help you maximize the value of your small business's assets. Asset Panda, a cloud-based asset tracking tool, can be used by businesses in many industries: education, healthcare, government, construction, and nonprofits, just to name a few. You can track physical items (like employee laptops and vehicle fleets) and digital assets (like software licenses or contracts) and have your histories, warranty information, and photos within one account. Through artificial intelligence, the tool can alert you about upcoming potential maintenance needs, underutilized assets, and an ideal life cycle for optimal asset value.

Investments

Offering retirement plans can attract new talent and differentiate you from competitors. If starting an employee investment and retirement plan is intimidating, check out Wealthfront, a financial tool known for its automated investing strategies. While Wealthfront uses sophisticated algorithms to manage investment portfolios, it tailors the portfolios based on each employee's risk tolerance, goals, and time horizon. The service automatically rebalances the allocation of assets in each portfolio, keeping the individual's preferences in mind, and employs tax-loss harvesting to optimize for taxes. It's an advanced automated investment feature for employees, leveraging technology to enhance the investment process.

Tax Compliance

We've established how artificial intelligence can help you with bookkeeping. AI technology can also help your small business navigate the complexities and ever-changing regulations around corporate taxes. By using artificial intelligence tools for tax compliance, you can:

- Reduce complexities by staying compliant without hiring additional human accounting experts.
- Minimize errors by ensuring tax rules are applied correctly to your calculations.
- Optimize tax advantages by reviewing your business's financial practices.
- Constantly stay compliant, even as regulations change over time.

There are multiple AI-powered accounting solutions on the market, and your business might even be using one now; powerhouse software like QuickBooks, TurboTax, H&R Block, Xero, and Zoho Books all have artificial intelligence features. FlyFin is another one previously mentioned that I've used personally and partnered with before. Additional lesser-known tax tools include Avalara, which specializes in sales tax compliance, and Wave Accounting, which streamlines tax filing with AI-driven income and expense tracking.

AI BRINGS EASE TO SMALL BUSINESS FINANCES

Artificial intelligence is an unparalleled asset for small businesses' finances. You don't need to be a large corporation to achieve financial success. You don't need to hire more bookkeepers. You don't need to categorize expenses manually. You don't need to be familiar with the latest tax regulations, and you don't even need to use financial spreadsheets! Artificial intelligence can do it all while giving you accurate analyses of your business's financial health.

I know how hard it can be to take your hands off the steering wheel, but trust me, once AI is in the driver's seat, you'll realize what you've been missing. You'll never have to worry about your financial reporting because AI can meticulously manage every detail. You and your team members will have more—in time and energy—to dedicate to customers, creativity, and business growth. And, with real-time financial data always at your fingertips, you can rest easy knowing that a financial miscalculation or mismanaged budget won't blindside you.

Artificial intelligence helps your small business operate with the financial savviness of a major corporation—without requiring a large financial team. You'll guess less, and you'll be free to strategize more. I can't wait for you to reap the many benefits of artificial intelligence for your business's finances.

Chapter 8

AI + Operations and Logistics

A rtificial intelligence's data insights, analysis, automation, and forecasting abilities all converge when it comes to small business operations and logistics. Human error? Gone. Demand forecasting? Consider it done—with precision. Seasonal business? Artificial intelligence has it handled. Overproduction? Say goodbye to that risk if you have AI involved.

Industries that might be particularly interested in using artificial intelligence for operations and logistics include transportation (using AI to optimize your routes, manage freights, and predict potential supply chain disruptions); healthcare (AI can predict equipment you might need, pharmacy stock levels, and other supply management needs); manufacturing (using AI to fully optimize your production schedule, anticipate maintenance needs, and handle quality control); food and beverage (to anticipate demand, optimize supply chains, reduce waste, and ensure fresh product delivery); and energy and utilities (to anticipate potential equipment failures and also efficiently distribute resources).

This chapter will review key components of operations and logistics to consider for your business and will include specific tools for various functions.

COMMON APPROACHES TO OPERATIONS

Operations and logistics are the systems and processes that move your business functions from point A to point B. By refining these, you can improve your business's output, satisfy customers, increase your bandwidth, and improve profitability. Mastering this part of your business is crucial so that you can repair what's not working and augment what is—and artificial intelligence can help you with almost every aspect.

There are several traditional approaches to operations, each having pros and cons depending on the business.

Just-in-Time (JIT)

Traditionally, JIT is used as an inventory management strategy that reduces waste and, as a result, saves money. This approach involves fine-tuning the receipt of goods within your production workflow to be precisely when needed, leading to lower inventory levels and decreased potential for waste. For example, my client Designers Resource Collection (DRC), the largest network of multiline showrooms on the West Coast, harnesses JIT principles in coordination with their manufacturers for creating custom-made furniture and decor. Instead of keeping a large inventory, DRC collaborates closely with their producers, who then order materials like fabric, metal, and wood based on the actual customer orders DRC compiles through their online platform. This method ensures that the manufacturing materials reflect current trends and customer preferences, effectively reducing unnecessary stock and minimizing surplus materials. Through this JIT approach, DRC facilitates the efficient production of furniture, directly aligning with customer specifications and design desires.

Try a variation of this prompt:

 Hi, I'm Natasha from Designers Resource Collection (DRC), the largest network of multiline showrooms on the West Coast. We specialize in creating custom-made furniture and decor, coordinating closely with manufacturers to apply just-in-time (JIT) principles. This approach allows us to order materials like fabric, metal, and wood based directly on actual customer orders we compile through our online platform, reducing unnecessary stock and minimizing surplus materials. Given our business model and desire to stay current with trends and customer preferences while managing our inventory efficiently, we're looking to integrate technology that can further streamline our JIT process. We aim to enhance our collaboration with producers, improve the accuracy of our material ordering, and gain better insights into inventory management. Currently, we coordinate these efforts through a combination of our Shopify site, which integrates with our inventory management system, and direct communication with our suppliers. What technology or tools would you recommend to optimize our JIT strategy, ensuring we maintain low inventory levels without compromising the ability to meet customer demands promptly? We're open to solutions that can seamlessly integrate with Shopify or offer significant improvements.

 Given the specific needs and operational model of Designers Resource Collection (DRC) as described, integrating technology to streamline your JIT process requires a solution that enhances collaboration, improves material ordering accuracy, and provides deep insights into inventory management. Here are a few recommendations:

- **Advanced ERP Systems:** Consider enterprise resource planning (ERP) systems that are specifically tailored for inventory management and can integrate seamlessly with manufacturing processes. Look for ERP solutions that offer robust modules for supply chain management, inventory control, and customer relationship management (CRM). These systems can automate the procurement process based on real-time sales data, helping you maintain optimal inventory levels. Some ERP systems are designed to work well with industries focusing on custom-made products and can integrate with your existing platforms like your online platform for order compilation.

- **Supply Chain Management Software:** Software solutions focused on supply chain management can offer specialized tools for managing JIT inventory. These tools can help you forecast demand more accurately, plan your procurement process, and optimize communication with your suppliers. They can also provide analytics to understand trends and customer preferences better, ensuring that your ordering process is as efficient as possible.

- **AI and Machine-Learning Tools:** AI and machine-learning algorithms can analyze historical data and predict future trends, helping you make more informed decisions about when and how much material to order. These tools can integrate with your current systems to provide predictive analytics for demand forecasting, inventory optimization, and trend analysis, allowing you to adjust your JIT strategy proactively.

- **Collaboration Platforms:** To enhance your collaboration with producers, consider tools that offer real-time communication, project management, and document sharing capabilities. Platforms like Slack, Microsoft Teams, or industry-specific collaboration tools can improve the efficiency of your communication with suppliers, ensuring that materials are ordered and delivered in a timely manner.

- **Custom Integration Solutions:** Given the unique aspects of your business, developing a custom solution that integrates directly with QuickBooks, Buildertrend, or your specific online platform may provide the most seamless experience. A custom-developed tool can be tailored to your specific workflow, incorporating JIT principles, inventory management, and supplier collaboration in one cohesive system.

When choosing technology or tools, consider factors such as compatibility with your existing systems, ease of use, scalability, and the ability to provide real-time insights and analytics. It may also be beneficial to consult with a technology provider who can offer a bespoke solution that addresses all your specific needs and challenges, ensuring that your JIT strategy is as efficient and effective as possible.

Artificial intelligence's predictive analytics can supercharge the JIT approach. Its machine-learning algorithms can accurately anticipate demand by observing your business's historical performance while considering external factors like market conditions and stockouts. Instead of manually reconfiguring schedules and inventory during a supply chain disruption, the AI can handle all of this for your business by adjusting production schedules and suggesting alternative suppliers for your needs.

Six Sigma

Six Sigma is a data-based methodology that isolates and repairs defects through a systematized set of steps. By following its DMAIC (Define, Measure, Analyze, Improve, Control) steps, businesses can effectively pinpoint problems and improve their business efficiency. The approach is instrumental in manufacturing and business processes because data (as opposed to a gut feeling) is used as the driving decision-maker in what needs to be done.

Artificial intelligence directly supports Six Sigma by constantly analyzing data—in a much more efficient and precise way than a human can. AI systems can monitor production data around the clock and note any discrepancies that deviate from standard practices. Through its machine-learning models, artificial intelligence can determine potential issues before they happen, akin to fortune-telling in the Six Sigma world.

Kanban

You might have noticed kanban layout options in software like Monday.com and Trello. The term refers to a visual task management system involving columns named for each process stage. (For example, at my agency we have: To-Do, In-Progress, Internal Approval, Client Review, Done, and On Hold as our kanban board column titles.) The system is helpful for visually seeing the status of tasks from a bird's-eye view, where the end goal is to move everything through to the complete column.

When you merge artificial intelligence with kanban, it adds a new level of automation that frees up team members even further. Instead of having someone responsible for moving each task through the kanban process (or, worse, trying to organize tasks that weren't updated), AI can update production flows in real time, automatically moving the tasks to each stage. In a packed kanban board, each column has a list of tasks, but no prioritization indicator exists. Artificial intelligence elevates kanban a step further by prioritizing tasks based on available resources and overall urgency, and it can also predict bottlenecks when a staff member or a product is unavailable in the future.

PREFERRED PLATFORMS FOR OPERATIONS

- **Connecteam.** While not explicitly an AI-driven platform, Connecteam offers robust features that significantly benefit operations and logistics, particularly for non-desk workforces. Its location tracking capabilities enable real-time monitoring of employees, ensuring efficient route management. For example, a logistics company can use Connecteam to streamline communication between dispatchers and drivers, monitor the progress of deliveries, and respond promptly to any logistical challenges that arise.
- **Blue Yonder.** Blue Yonder provides supply chain management software powered by artificial intelligence. Its machine-learning abilities support businesses in optimizing their operations to drive growth. From predicting demand to fulfilling orders to mastering customer experiences, the tool has supported more than three thousand brands in making smarter decisions with their operations and logistics.

FINDING OPPORTUNITIES FOR AI WITHIN YOUR EXISTING SYSTEMS

When artificial intelligence can do (almost) anything and everything, knowing where to start can be overwhelming, particularly if you're inserting the technology into your existing operational and logistical systems. Go through the following questions to narrow down the opportunities for your company. Bonus points: Have one to two teammates repeat the same exercise and compare your notes.

1. Do you collect data across your operations and logistics? If so, where does it go, and what do you track?
2. How do you evaluate and analyze your operational and logistical data?
3. What challenges are you facing when managing or fulfilling inventory or services?

4. Do you have real-time knowledge of every part of your supply chain?
5. If a supply chain element is disrupted, how do you identify and fix it? How long does this take collectively?
6. How do you anticipate customer demand?
7. What are you delivering quickly to your clients or customers?
8. What are you delivering inefficiently to your clients or customers?
9. How do you predict what your customers want for goods or services?
10. What are the top three bottlenecks in your business?
11. What is your quality control process, and can it be improved?
12. When was the last time you experienced downtime that impacted your business operations? What happened and why?
13. How do you determine where to allocate human workers and material resources?
14. How do you monitor compliance, particularly keeping up with regulations and managing risk?
15. How do you keep up with market trends and consumer behavior?
16. What are the top five most repetitive tasks that could be automated in your operations or logistics?
17. Are decisions made on instincts or data within your company? If data, what data are you using for your choices?
18. Are you prepared for a spontaneous major operational or logistical disruption? What would that look like?

These questions are meant to expose potential weaknesses in your overall business functions. If this exercise made you panicky about how much work needs to be done, don't worry. Choose only one to three items to focus on for now. Once artificial intelligence is in your court, you can correct more areas of weakness.

Automate Procurement and Fulfillment

What AI can do: Avoid surpluses and shortages by analyzing data and market trends so you have the proper stock on hand.

Recommended AI tools for this task: Kensho, Locus Robotics, Shipwell

Data you might need on hand: Historical sales data, inventory levels, supplier information, market trends and forecasts, shipping and logistics data

If your business sells physical goods, then you know how critical procurement and fulfillment can be for success; artificial intelligence can help you with both of these business operations. And if your business doesn't sell physical goods, this section will still be useful to you and might even inspire more ideas about using artificial intelligence in your business.

Procurement is the process of obtaining or receiving the goods and services necessary for your business to fulfill its overall operations. Generally, procurement can be broken down into the following components:

- Sourcing, or identifying various suppliers who can get you the goods or services your business needs to do its work.
- Negotiating to finalize purchase terms, such as payment, timing, and delivery.
- Ordering goods or services under the agreed terms.
- Receiving, including accepting and inspecting the goods to make sure they meet the quality standards of your agreement.
- Managing a continued good relationship with your suppliers.

Fulfillment is everything after procurement; it's when you get the product to the customer after a sale. Warehousing inventory, packaging, shipping, handling, and returns all fall into this bucket. Most businesses have a similar goal: efficiently getting high-quality products or services to customers with minimal extra costs. In a specific breakdown:

- Warehousing and storing your goods so you can quickly access the items after an order is placed.
- Processing or preparing the order for delivery—you pick up the item and package it.
- Shipping and sending the product to the customer after evaluating an optimal shipping method.
- Communicating with the customer about their order, including customer service for basic inquiries, complaints, and returns.

Procurement and fulfillment are necessary functionalities for any business. Companies can proactively adjust procurement operations and strategy with artificial intelligence's predictive analytics. Instead of having too much inventory or not enough, AI avoids surpluses and shortages by analyzing data and market trends so you have the proper stock on hand. AI's automation abilities also extend to the procurement of physical goods. If an item needs replenishment, AI can automatically place an order, ultimately saving you or a team member hours of analysis and communication for even a single item.

You might be thinking, "This is all great. AI can handle inventory management, so now my team and I can work on supplier selection and management!" Well, hold your horses—artificial intelligence can help on that front too. AI can help you evaluate suppliers based on past performance and market conditions, and it can help you find partners who will be reliable in good and bad times.

On the fulfillment side of things, artificial intelligence is truly genius in action through automation. From using AI-driven robots to sort and pick packed goods to using AI to optimize delivery routes, artificial intelligence can almost entirely handle your warehouse fulfillment process from start to finish.

Preferred Platforms for Procurement

Try these tools to help with your procurement and fulfillment needs:

- **Kensho.** An advanced analytics tool with data-driven insights, Kensho's artificial intelligence technology uses predictive analytics to clearly depict market demand and trends. Its machine-learning algorithms review datasets to identify patterns, helping businesses proactively manage their inventory.
- **Locus Robotics.** This company provides autonomous mobile robots (AMRs) to warehouses, where they can move stored items to packing areas. Each robot has a user-friendly interface, so your staff can interact with, provide commands to, and bring them right into the warehouse workflow.
- **Shipwell.** Shipwell's artificial intelligence leans on machine learning to maximize shipping and delivery routes. Its AI analyzes weather, traffic, and delivery windows to suggest the best shipping routes and prioritize fuel saving. Shipwell has a real-time dashboard to track outbound shipments, allowing you to pull up-to-the-minute order statuses for inquiring customers.

Manage Your Supply Chain

What AI can do: Find suppliers, anticipate orders, and suggest savings opportunities.

Recommended AI tools for this task: Scoutbee, Prevedere, IBM Food Trust, SAP Business Network for Logistics, SAP Integrated Business Planning for Supply Chain (SAP IBP)

Data you might need on hand: Supplier information, inventory levels, sales data, market trends, logistics data, quality control metrics, cost data

A single hurdle in your supply chain could seriously hinder your business. Do any of these situations feel familiar to you?

- You feel like you're either overstocked or sold out all the time.
- You find it hard to predict future demand with accuracy.
- You manage your inventory manually.
- You miss out on opportunities for bulk purchasing discounts because you aren't sure of your inventory levels.
- You spend days selecting and managing your suppliers.
- You have challenges identifying bottlenecks.
- You feel disorganized with tracking shipments.
- You worry about a single disruption completely halting your business's supply chain.
- You make efficiency decisions based on "hunches" instead of data.
- You know you're spending excessively on shipping, warehousing, and manual labor, but you lack time to fix it.
- You always feel "behind the times" on regulatory standards and quality control.
- You worry about customer satisfaction and see many complaints come in.

If any of those items started making your palms sweat, here's the good news: Artificial intelligence can help with each and every one of those common supply chain management issues for small businesses.

If you need support sourcing, evaluating, and managing suppliers, artificial intelligence can be an effective "second brain" to improve an existing vertical or even make one from scratch. Let's say a clothing boutique owner wants to create an exclusive in-house clothing line of eco-friendly apparel. Instead of combing through global textile suppliers from scratch and then manually evaluating each on a variety of factors, artificial intelligence can help narrow down the preliminary search. A tool like Scoutbee harnesses artificial intelligence to manage suppliers, making it far easier to organize and track different vendors. Within their intelligence platform, their AI can help users efficiently find potential suppliers while identifying procurement risks. Not only will you have up-to-the-moment information about your preferred suppliers; you'll also save immense amounts of time with research and management—which can instead be applied to bringing the idea to fruition.

Artificial intelligence can predict disruptions that might affect produce supply for a business like a local grocery store chain that is impacted by seasonality, with a tool like Prevedere, an AI-powered predictive planning tool. With AI as part of the store team, management would receive alerts about potential weather or seasonal issues. Then, the store can adjust the orders well in advance, essentially bypassing the obstacle. With AI, a potential disaster becomes "business as usual," saving your team from scrambling and your customers from disappointment.

For many businesses with a supply chain, transparency and traceability are critical. When multiple raw materials and products are coming from different sources, small businesses need to know where these materials are coming from, if those materials meet their standards, and when they can expect those materials to arrive. A craft brewery must track hops, grains, yeast, specialty ingredients (like fruit, spices, and herbs), additives and chemicals, and packaging materials (like bottles, cans, kegs, and labels). A single batch of beer may require knowledge of at least nine ingredients and materials in order to make a sellable product. Tools like IBM Food Trust or SAP Business Network for Logistics have AI-based solutions that track the movement of each supply chain element. The tools also use blockchain technology, which essentially gives a transaction record of every process in the product's journey. What's really cool here is that the brewery could then use that information to enlighten consumers on the sourced elements of their beverage.

For a company that makes bicycles, they'll need to consider not only all the different parts to make the bike—frames, chains, and tires—but also the number of bikes sold. Each bike is going to require different parts—tires or different sizes of frames. If the company offers different bike upgrades, that also adds another element of complexity to the equation. Artificial intelligence can help make sense of the inventory needs by monitoring (a) how many bikes are sold, (b) what types of bikes are sold, and (c) the specific parts needed to hold an optimal inventory level. And beyond ordering parts, artificial intelligence can predict production scheduling—what bikes should be made when—and coordinate this information with the suppliers. A tool like SAP Integrated Business Planning for Supply Chain (SAP IBP) is like a smart assistant that monitors, analyzes, predicts, and manages.

AI in Practice

I am extraordinarily proud of the clients I've worked with, and Dr. Lora Shahine is no exception. Lora is a reproductive endocrinologist who's on a mission to shatter stigmas about pregnancy loss and miscarriage. She has inspired thousands of people across her TikTok, Instagram, and YouTube accounts by bringing the masses transparency and education about fertility.

As a reproductive endocrinologist at Pacific NW Fertility in Seattle, Lora provides fertility treatments to help people achieve their goals of having a baby. The fertility center is known for its state-of-the-art technology and personalized patient experience. As such, Lora spends most days providing back-to-back patient care, from initial consultations to embryo transfers.

The complexities of operating a fertility clinic are overwhelming to say the least. Almost every facet of providing fertility treatment is carefully timed. For people with ovaries, fertility testing is often based on different stages of their menstrual cycle, where hormone levels are tested during specific windows that can sometimes be mere days long. Procedures like egg retrievals, intrauterine insemination (IUI), and in vitro fertilization (IVF) must happen during exact periods of a person's cycle, and the consequences of being a day off can often mean delaying treatment by another month. Multiply these factors by patients undergoing different treatment stages, each with their menstrual cycle times, and you can see how difficult it could be to juggle the clinic's schedule.

As I always recommend, it's helpful first to isolate the primary challenges you'd like artificial intelligence to address. With Lora's fertility clinic, there are seemingly limitless ways AI could help increase efficiencies, predict demand, and help with patients, so to reduce overwhelm, here's what I would advise Lora:

1. Master and Maximize Patient Treatment Scheduling

As mentioned, every patient's menstrual cycle is unique, and procedures like fertility testing, egg retrievals, embryo transfers, and intrauterine insemination need to happen at precise points in an individual's cycle. With artificial intelligence's help, patients' cycle data could be analyzed in depth. Instead of manually calendaring when specific treatments should take place, artificial intelligence could predict the best times for particular treatments and automate the scheduling.

In real time and with every patient, artificial intelligence could use machine learning to drive the necessary staff and resource allocation to help the maximum number of patients. Its predictive capabilities would consider the potential treatment schedule, then tally up the number of procedures, classify the types of procedures—egg retrieval or insemination, for example—and then apply the ideal treatment time windows across the patients' menstrual cycles. From there, artificial intelligence could forecast Pacific NW Fertility's required resources and even predict peak times when additional staff are needed.

Beyond anticipating what treatments need to happen and when, artificial intelligence could optimize staff schedules, ensuring adequate nurses and doctors are available without being overworked. Pacific NW Fertility would have forecasted treatment times, and there would be buffer times for patient preparation and follow-up. And, if someone needs to move their appointment, it would be no problem: AI could automatically adjust staff schedules as appointments are rescheduled, ensuring optimal resource allocation for the clinic.

As if the scheduling wasn't great enough, AI could also communicate the schedules to all, including staff and patient reminders about appointments, notifications of schedule changes, pretreatment preparation instructions, and more.

I should note that, for something this tailored, Lora would want to contact IBM Watson Health (previously mentioned) to develop a custom AI solution. This way, Pacific NW Fertility could have artificial intelligence that works best for the clinic's needs, from patient data all the way through staffing requirements.

2. Educate and Retain Patients

Seeking fertility treatment can be a tough and emotional road. When patients come to see Lora, they're often in a place of grieving—for the family they desire, for the pregnancies they've lost, for the life plans they might not have. When patients finally come to see Lora, they have often been trying to have a baby for six or more months, and while Pacific NW Fertility moves fast, the process can still take months due to the cyclical nature of getting pregnant.

Lora believes in the power of education, and having detailed data points about her clinic's fertility statistics could help her manage her patients' expectations. With the help of artificial intelligence, Lora would have real-time data about her clinic's many moving pieces, including the percentage of successful pregnancies, the typical timeline of patients for various treatments, the average number of transfers, and more.

Additionally, artificial intelligence could provide Lora with data from past patients, like trends in treatment paths, the outcomes of those treatments, and other timeline details. After analysis, the AI tool could identify patterns and correlations, notifying Lora of potential new observations. This detailed analysis could populate a personalized timeline for each patient and allow for Lora to review various procedures and milestones, ranging from initial fertility testing to embryo transfer. The timelines could also adjust dynamically based on the latest patient data, the bandwidth of the clinic, and the patient's progress in treatment.

Artificial intelligence can also provide patients with information outside the timeline to ensure they feel supported and cared for between appointments. The AI platform could generate relevant educational content for that patient's treatment phase, for emotional support, and more. From an emotional standpoint, an AI-powered tool could regularly check in to see if they have questions or concerns and then escalate any complex inquiries to staff.

3. Improve Data Analysis for Treatment Plans

Much of infertility is unexplained. Sometimes, even with the best fertility testing and the best fertility treatments by the best physicians, people are unable to become pregnant. While Pacific NW Fertility is high performing by national standards, the practice might benefit from artificial intelligence's insights about the industry to optimize treatments even more. With artificial intelligence in Lora's tool kit, she could rely on AI as an extra set of eyes, particularly when recommending treatment plans.

As we know, artificial intelligence could help synthesize the clinic's outcomes at a general level; but AI can also drill down to an individual level. Artificial intelligence can interpret data from patient fertility tests—sperm analysis, ovarian reserve levels, and more—to identify correlations and patterns from previous successful treatment plans. From there, artificial intelligence's machine-learning algorithms can forecast various treatment outcomes for that individual patient, using clinic-wide treatment data to recommend what treatment path will most likely result in a successful pregnancy. As an example, artificial intelligence could analyze a couple's fertility test results, medical histories, and other factors to suggest bypassing IUI (typically the first treatment plan) and going straight to IVF. Or, artificial intelligence could review a couple's genetic markers to find an egg donor match that reduces the risk of genetic conditions.

With artificial intelligence carrying the brunt of data tracking, analysis, and projections, Lora and Pacific NW Fertility would have more bandwidth for patients and for keeping up with the latest fertility treatment technology. Lora and her team could feel confident about providing patients with the best possible treatment plans because the recommendations are individualized and based on thousands of historical data points.

FINAL THOUGHTS

If you genuinely want to improve your business operations and logistics, I strongly encourage you to use artificial intelligence. Through AI, you can get a comprehensive summary of every stop along your supply chain, allowing you to have insight into what's working and what can be improved. Artificial intelligence's predictive capabilities help you anticipate potential problems, ensuring your business operates without a hitch amid setbacks while still satisfying customers.

Chapter 9

AI + Human Resources and Talent Management

There's a saying that goes something like, "You're only as strong as your weakest team member." I'd argue that you're only as strong as your weakest artificial intelligence tool. And businesses that aren't using a tool? They're only experiencing a fraction of the strength they could be as an organization. As a small business owner, you want to be able to maximize your business in every way. AI makes this goal possible.

Today's digital era moves fast, and leveraging human capital is critical for companies that want to grow. Yes, artificial intelligence can help with many administrative tasks, but your business can only go so far without the right combination of skills, creativity, and commitment from human team members. I firmly believe that the successful organizations of tomorrow will have a synergistic relationship with artificial intelligence, where AI will shoulder routine and data-intense tasks so human workers can operate from a place of creativity. This chapter will explore the many ways you can use artificial intelligence to build and fortify the human components of your small business. You'll learn about AI tools that can directly improve your company's capabilities in attracting and retaining the best talent possible.

EMPOWER HUMAN CAPITAL WITH AI

By now, you know that this book doesn't view artificial intelligence as a threat to humans; rather, it is a complementary force. When humans and technology combine, the collaboration can lead to greatness, particularly in organizational culture. Without artificial intelligence, human resources work in companies is time intensive and manual. From processing payroll to setting up company benefits to approving vacation requests, working in HR can be a slippery slope of paper pushing. Without artificial intelligence, it's easy for administrative tasks to squash the *human* part of human resources.

If you have a team member in human resources, they're likely exemplary at creating connections and seeing individual potential. Their area of genius is probably not in filling out forms, processing sick leave, or summarizing complex 401(k) policies. Their strengths lie in *people*, and artificial intelligence can free them up to focus on their best talents.

To be clear, I'm not implying that administrative work is unimportant. Having written policies and approvals is essential for a functioning business. But administrative work doesn't necessarily need to be done by a human. Artificial intelligence's rapid-speed data processing and automation abilities are more efficient and precise than humans. With today's technology, it simply doesn't make sense to have your organization's most people-savvy workers spend time on paperwork when they could create a thriving work environment instead.

HOW AI CAN ASSIST HUMAN RESOURCES FUNCTIONS

Whether you have an HR team or a business of one, I bet there are at least three human resources–related tasks you must contend with regularly. Think of a repeating task you do more than five times a month that you'd like to review and consider using AI to help. Here are a few ideas to start:

- Screening resumes for a job listing.
- Narrowing down potential candidates, whether it's through a professional network or on a job board.

- Conducting screening interviews for job candidates.
- Scheduling interview times between job candidates and interviewers at your company.
- Running criminal background checks on job candidates.
- Onboarding new employees on company policies and culture.
- Saving employee-signed documents and contracts related to their role.
- Scheduling exit interviews.
- Analyzing exit interviews.
- Revoking access after an employee leaves your company.
- Updating an employee's personal details, such as marital status or mailing address.
- Approving employee personal, sick, and vacation days.
- Processing payroll, including tax withholdings.
- Enrolling employees in your health insurance and retirement plan benefits.
- Collecting 360-degree feedback from colleagues for performance reviews.
- Collecting self-assessments for performance reviews.
- Tracking progress toward goals, both at an individual and team level.
- Distributing assessments for specific skills before hiring or promoting.
- Researching courses and learning opportunities for different roles.
- Sharing online training materials.
- Recording employee certifications and renewal dates.
- Distributing and analyzing employee satisfaction surveys.
- Managing employee recognition and rewards programs.
- Monitoring regulatory compliance in employment laws.
- Tracking workforce diversity and inclusion metrics.
- Reporting on turnover rates, hiring velocity, and cost per hire.
- Managing desk and office space assignments.

Each of these tasks could eat up hours per year (if not per month!) in time. By employing artificial intelligence, your HR workers will be freed up to think strategically about your organizational culture, employees, and overall company performance.

PREFERRED PLATFORM FOR HUMAN RESOURCES

Here is a list of AI tools I recommend to human resources departments:

- **Sessions.** Sessions, to me, is a great alternative to Zoom. It has many great features, including its AI Copilot, which replaces the need for a manual notetaker, freeing your participants to engage fully without worrying about missing notes. The tool has a built-in agenda feature, making it easy to stay on track, and its AI Copilot can insert polls to meeting participants. The AI Copilot also does live transcriptions (including who said what) with time stamps, and it can summarize the meeting discussion with action items.

Recruit and Staff

What AI can do: Quickly review candidates, assess cultural fit through predictive analytics, streamline interview scheduling, and automate initial screening processes.

Recommended AI tools for this task: LinkedIn Recruiter, Entelo, Plum, Eightfold, Lever, HireVue, Greenhouse, GoodTime, Checkr

Data you might need on hand: Job description and necessary qualifications, candidate information, assessment data, interview process data, other onboarding information

It may feel contradictory, but recruiting is based on evaluating data points. Your job posting details the ideal features of your candidate, and then every candidate is put through a series of evaluations until you make a hire. From the information on their resume to the interview process, we all subconsciously run the candidate through a series of filters to determine the best fit for the role.

Artificial intelligence creates organization behind those subconscious data points that HR specialists apply to the recruiting process. With artificial intelligence, your small business can experience a transformative shift in the way you hire. You will no longer have to review hundreds of resumes to find the best fit manually. Artificial intelligence can do this for you and, through its comprehensive data analysis skills, ensure you don't accidentally pass over your dream candidate.

AI in Practice

My client Michele Plachter could benefit from artificial intelligence when hiring for her rapidly growing interior design firm. Michele is the founder and CEO of Michele Plachter Design (MPD), a Philadelphia-based interior design firm specializing in luxury interiors. Due to demand, her firm has expanded to the Fort Lauderdale area. Given the high-end nature of the firm's clientele, new employees must have tangible client management skills while possessing strong creative judgment. Let's review how Michele can use AI to help her find the perfect candidates.

Efficiently Identify Candidates

Integrating artificial intelligence could strongly support MPD's recruitment process. AI could help widen the pool of potential candidates, streamline a vetting process, and ensure they retain the best talent to support the firm's goals and reputation for excellence.

LinkedIn Recruiter and Entelo are AI-powered recruitment tools with automated search functions. If Michele needs a new interior designer, she or a team member would create accounts on these platforms and enter their new hire requirements. These requirements can range from highly specific (like possessing certain degrees or certifications) to experience-based (five years or more of working in luxury interior design) to any other qualities aligning with their firm's culture. After the job requirements are inserted, AI works its magic, comparing MPD's job posting to a robust database with thousands of professionals. The artificial intelligence will proactively seek all potential candidates, not just those seeking employment, ensuring no stone is left unturned.

Once artificial intelligence completes its search, Michele will receive a list of candidates for the role. Imagine how many hours of manual searching this could save! With a few details and a click of a button, MPD has a vetted list of matches.

Through Entelo, a recruiting automation platform, Michele can leverage predictive algorithms and data-backed insights to streamline the candidate discovery and engagement process. While Entelo may not specifically assess the creative quality of candidates' design work, it excels in identifying candidates whose experience and skills align with the firm's requirements. Michele can use Entelo to source candidates efficiently, benefiting from its extensive recruiting data to ensure a more innovative, faster hiring process. It allows for direct communication with potential candidates, enhancing Michele's ability to find talent that meets the firm's standards.

In conjunction with Entelo, Michele can also utilize Huntica for the initial screening phase. Huntica's AI-driven platform specializes in analyzing resumes and matching candidates to job descriptions based on specific criteria. By scoring and ranking candidates, Huntica helps Michele quickly identify top talent that fits the firm's exact requirements, further optimizing the selection process before moving forward with more in-depth evaluations.

If the candidates show interest in the role, Michele can continue to use artificial intelligence to support the interviewing process. A tool like Plum or Eightfold would be beneficial for determining cultural fit. These AI-powered assessments can assess if the candidate is a good match personally and professionally, because she wants to hire someone who will stay with her company and enjoy the work experience. Michele and her team could also specify what traits they value most (like being collaborative in a work environment), and the tools would highlight the candidates who most strongly exhibit these traits.

Preferred Platforms for Recruiting

Here are some tools you can try to help with recruiting:

- **Lever.** Lever is a comprehensive recruiting platform that combines an applicant tracking system (ATS) and candidate relationship management (CRM). It has thousands of customers across industries like media and entertainment, healthcare, consumer technology, retail and e-commerce, and SaaS.
- **HireVue.** HireVue is an end-to-end hiring tool that assesses candidates based on filmed video responses. By sending out the same interview questions to all candidates, HireVue hopes to level the playing field to mitigate any potential bias from an in-person interview with varying questions.
- **Greenhouse.** Greenhouse is a hiring operating system trusted by companies like Squarespace, J.D. Power, Harry's, Wayfair, and HubSpot. Greenhouse uses artificial intelligence to create an equitable experience for candidates by reducing bias that might result from human-driven searches.
- **GoodTime.** GoodTime is an AI-powered appointment scheduling tool specifically for interviewing job candidates. With millions of meetings scheduled, the tool has become a staple for companies like Box, Shopify, and Zoom.
- **Checkr.** Checkr uses AI for the background checking process when hiring by identifying and classifying a candidate's criminal charges across a real-time data network.
- **Huntica.** Huntica leverages AI to automate the screening process by analyzing candidate resumes and matching them with job descriptions. It ranks and scores candidates based on data-driven insights, helping recruiters quickly identify top talent and streamline the early stages of recruitment.

Even the most diligent and inclusive people are capable of subconscious bias during hiring. If a recruiter or hiring manager relies on "intuition," they might show unconscious favoritism to candidates with similar backgrounds, unintentionally limiting your organization from finding better-fitting candidates. There also might be stereotyping and prejudice at play, such as making assumptions about someone's work ethic based on their race, appearance, age, or gender. In an interview setting, the interviewer may ask leading questions that support their preconceived notion about the candidate, or the hiring manager may apply bias to nonverbal communication like body language or attire when evaluating a candidate's fit for a role.

Artificial intelligence can counteract these human biases by applying objective assessments and standardized candidate interview processes. Post-hiring, artificial intelligence's data analysis capabilities can ensure your organization continues to practice inclusion and diversity.

Diversity in Team Composition

AI tools can ensure bias-free candidate screening. Because of artificial intelligence's objective nature, tools can ignore factors irrelevant to an individual's capabilities—their name, gender, age, and race, for starters—so your candidates are screened based on skills and experience. Artificial intelligence also ensures your small business maximizes your candidate pool by seeking platforms where diverse candidates might be active.

Committing to diversity can start with your job description. Try your own version of the following exercise with a generative AI tool to cowrite a job posting that appeals to diverse candidates.

AI in Action

Try a variation of this prompt:

 I own a dental practice in Albuquerque, New Mexico, and I need help writing a job description. I need to hire a dental hygienist. I am committed to diversity, equity, and inclusion at my office, so please make sure the job posting does not have any biases and is appealing to a diverse pool of candidates.

 Creating an inclusive and unbiased job description for a dental hygienist role involves focusing on essential qualifications, responsibilities, and values without implying preferences that might deter diverse applicants. Here's a sample job description tailored to your needs:

Job Title: Dental Hygienist

Location: Albuquerque, New Mexico

About Us: At [Your Practice Name], we are committed to providing exceptional dental care to our community in Albuquerque, New Mexico. Our practice is built on the principles of excellence, compassion, and inclusivity. We believe in fostering a welcoming environment for both our patients and staff, embracing diversity, equity, and inclusion in all aspects of our operations. We are seeking a Dental Hygienist who shares our commitment to patient care and values working in a diverse and inclusive workplace.

Position Overview: The Dental Hygienist will play a crucial role in our team by providing high-quality dental hygiene treatments and patient education. We are looking for a dedicated professional who is passionate about oral health and committed to providing compassionate care to our diverse patient base.

Key Responsibilities: Conduct dental health assessments, including reviewing patient histories and performing oral health assessments.

Perform professional dental cleanings, apply preventive materials, and provide education on proper oral hygiene practices.

Work closely with the dental team to develop and implement personalized care plans for patients.

Ensure strict compliance with infection control and safety protocols.

Engage with patients in a manner that respects their diverse backgrounds and needs, ensuring a comfortable and positive dental care experience.

Qualifications: Associate degree or higher in Dental Hygiene from an accredited institution.

Valid Dental Hygienist license in the state of New Mexico.

CPR certification.

Excellent communication and interpersonal skills, with a focus on patient-centered care.

Commitment to continuing education and professional development.

We Offer: A supportive and inclusive work environment.

Opportunities for professional growth and development.

Competitive salary and benefits package.

A commitment to diversity, equity, and inclusion in the workplace.

How to Apply: Please submit your resume, cover letter, and any relevant certifications to [Your Email Address] with the subject line "Dental Hygienist Application." In your cover letter, we encourage you to share your experiences or commitments to diversity, equity, and inclusion.

[Your Practice Name] is an equal opportunity employer. We celebrate diversity and are committed to creating an inclusive environment for all employees. We encourage candidates of all backgrounds, experiences, abilities, and perspectives to apply.

*

This job description emphasizes your commitment to diversity, equity, and inclusion, focusing on the qualifications and responsibilities relevant to the role without introducing biases that could deter a diverse range of candidates.

Preferred Platforms for DEI

These platforms are especially helpful for diversity and equity initiatives:

- **Pymetrics.** Pymetrics describes itself as a soft skills platform. The tool's AI uses data-driven behavioral insights to bring a fair hiring process to candidates and companies. It sends gamified soft skill assessments to candidates that measure logical reasoning, risk tolerance, decision-making, attention, learning abilities, generosity, and more. As of writing, the tool decreases the average hiring time by 59%, and it led to a 62% increase in female representation among its customers.

- **Culture Amp.** Culture Amp is an employee engagement and performance tool that helps companies better understand their workers. Thousands of companies use the platform—including SoulCycle, Etsy, and McDonald's—to gather insights on the employee experience, including diversity and inclusion. The platform's artificial intelligence runs in-depth analytics reports to synthesize feedback, measure inclusivity, and track the effectiveness of your initiatives.

Committing to Diversity

Diversity is a strength that can supercharge your business in multiple ways. For example, you can attract a better talent pool, have a wider range of perspectives within your organization, enhance employee satisfaction, and much, much more.

Hiring diverse talent is the first of many steps in committing to an equitable workplace. Artificial intelligence lets your business monitor and report on DEI metrics in real time. You can get an immediate picture of your team's diversity, set diversity goals, monitor your progress toward those goals, and even go so far as visualizing those metrics. This type of analysis can uncover unconscious biases in your hiring or management processes so you can confront and rectify systemic barriers in every facet of your organization. Taking things a step further, employing this type of accountability can act as a positive feedback loop; if you broadcast your ongoing commitment to diversity through AI tools, you will create an environment that does indeed attract diverse talent.

Overcoming Bias in AI

Artificial intelligence is inherently unbiased because the technology measures data points. However, it is important to underscore that artificial intelligence can exhibit biases because of its machine-learning algorithms.

We know that AI learns from historical data points. If your business has had discriminatory (unconscious or conscious) practices, like promoting certain genders or races faster, then artificial intelligence may continue to make recommendations in favor of these past trends. Essentially, AI can reinforce existing biases if not managed carefully. Here are some strategies to mitigate any artificial intelligence prejudices:

- Always provide your AI systems with a wide range of examples across different demographics.
- Regularly audit and assess your AI for biases.
- Ensure that you and all stakeholders clearly understand the evaluation criteria used by AI for certain decisions.
- Promote diversity within the teams developing and managing the artificial intelligence systems.
- Frequently use bias detection and correction tools meant to mitigate prejudices within AI systems.
- Stay up-to-date with legal standards and best practices about discrimination and artificial intelligence.

Artificial intelligence is a tool; it's not a replacement for human intelligence. A commitment to diversity and inclusion means addressing bias in places you might never expect, and—with thoughtful guidance—artificial intelligence can help you build a more robust and more diverse company.

Train and Develop Employees

What AI can do: Create personalized courses to provide new and continuing training for employees.

Recommended AI tools for this task: PETE

Data you might need on hand: Employee profiles, learning preferences, course objectives and outcomes, company data, performance metrics, feedback mechanisms

Everyone has a unique way of learning. Since there's no one-size-fits-all solution for learning, artificial intelligence can address personalized learning opportunities that help the learner and, as a ripple effect, the company. With a tool like PETE, small businesses can create individually tailored courses through its AI-powered learning platform. For example, if you want to standardize your employee onboarding process, you could create a course with an overview of your company values, history, culture, benefits packages, and working structures. PETE's AI-powered course builder would help you create a description, pinpoint desired learning outcomes, compile resources, and weigh in on assessments to retain the information. The platform then creates video lessons with the instructor's likeness and voice, providing a learning environment conducive to visual learners. To cap it off, once the learner takes the course, PETE's AI technology will hyper-personalize the content to the learner, updating the course in real time.

Imagine how many hours of one-on-one training a tool like PETE could save your company! And, unlike when a human conducts training, PETE's AI technology can adjust the content delivery to maximize retention throughout the course, specific to that learner.

Leadership consultants can also use artificial intelligence to ensure and quantify the effectiveness of their training. My client and Brandmasters member Colleen DelVecchio, a certified CliftonStrengths coach, provides individual and group coaching sessions through her firm, Maxady. CliftonStrengths is a developmental tool that helps individuals identify their top five strengths out of thirty-four themes. Almost every strength combination is unique, and the order and combination of the top five strengths require nuance and understanding.

While Colleen is a pro, she could use artificial intelligence to do the heavy lifting of an initial CliftonStrengths analysis, and then apply her own touch to ensure the client is getting the best reading possible. Here's an example of how a generative AI tool would interpret my CliftonStrengths if Colleen were assessing me.

→ AI in Action

Try a variation of this prompt:

 I am a certified CliftonStrengths coach. I am meeting with my client Phil tomorrow to provide leadership training. His top five strengths in order are Positivity, Woo, Communication, Activator, and Maximizer. Please summarize what makes Phil unique and capable as a leader based on these strengths.

 Phil's CliftonStrengths profile suggests he has a powerful combination of interpersonal and motivational talents that make him uniquely capable as a leader. Here's a summary of what makes Phil unique and highlights his leadership capabilities:

- **Positivity:** Phil's Positivity means he has an infectious enthusiasm that can greatly enhance team morale and motivation. Leaders with this strength are often seen as a source of inspiration and motivation, able to keep the team's spirits high even in challenging times. Phil's optimistic outlook can help him see the best in people and situations, making it easier to navigate through difficulties with a positive attitude.

- **Woo (Winning Others Over):** Phil's Woo signifies his exceptional ability to connect with others. This strength makes him particularly adept at networking, building relationships, and persuading others. As a leader, this means Phil can effectively rally people to his cause, build strong alliances, and encourage a collaborative and inclusive team environment. His ability to win others over is crucial for leading diverse teams and driving change.

- **Communication:** With Communication as a top strength, Phil has a natural ability to articulate ideas, vision, and values in a way that is engaging and understandable. This strength enables him to be an effective spokesperson for his team or organization, inspire and motivate through storytelling, and ensure clear and open lines of communication within his team. Leaders with strong communication skills are often more effective at resolving conflicts, setting expectations, and guiding their teams toward common goals.

- **Activator:** Phil's Activator strength indicates he is naturally inclined to turn thoughts into action. Leaders with this strength are often catalysts for change, able to initiate projects and motivate others to move from planning to execution quickly. Phil's ability to start things can be instrumental in driving progress and achieving results, making him well suited to fast-paced or entrepreneurial environments where agility and rapid implementation are valued.

- **Maximizer:** Phil's Maximizer strength suggests he has a keen eye for leveraging strengths in himself and others to achieve excellence. He is likely to focus on refining and building on existing talents within his team rather than trying to correct weaknesses. This approach encourages individuals to excel in their areas of strength. Phil's ability to identify and cultivate the potential in his team members can significantly enhance team effectiveness and productivity.

Overall, Phil's combination of strengths positions him as a leader who is not only adept at inspiring and motivating his team but also skilled in building relationships, communicating effectively, initiating action, and striving for excellence. His leadership style is likely to be dynamic, inclusive, and focused on leveraging the best in people to achieve outstanding results.

For a group workshop, Colleen could use generative AI to analyze everyone's strengths in the room, allowing her to tailor her content pre-emptively. She could also use AI-powered survey tools before and after the workshop to observe behavioral or performance changes. Using AI to provide data-driven designs maximizes the organization's return on investment and also helps Colleen deliver content based on AI's observations. Win-win.

Preferred Platforms for Training

Here are some tools to try for help in tailoring your content to your employees:

- **Lattice.** Lattice fuses artificial intelligence with people management to create an experience that maximizes career development among workers. The tool can tailor its content to give recommendations to both the manager and the employee, helping both parties be on the same page about the individual's development.
- **Bonusly.** Think of this artificial intelligence tool to gamify employee recognition. Bonusly's technology combines data analysis and natural language processing to create personalized rewards that result in higher worker satisfaction and productivity.
- **Zenefits.** Zenefits's artificial intelligence automates manual human resources tasks. From benefits administration to payroll to compliance, the AI tool uses data processing and machine learning to personalize to-dos while making predictions about HR-related decisions like employee benefits and company policies.

- **Gusto.** Gusto's AI integrations save hours of manual HR data prep, particularly relating to salaries and deductions, while also providing ample reporting options. The artificial intelligence also monitors tax laws, providing automatic updates to ensure compliance.
- **Visier.** Visier's artificial intelligence predicts workforce trends and provides benchmark data from over two hundred million data points from other companies. Visier's AI helps see where you fall against the competition regarding your employees' compensations and career development paths.

AI: THE STRATEGIC ADVANTAGE OF HUMAN RESOURCES

The capabilities of artificial intelligence profoundly change how we work with people. Through AI, human resources professionals and small businesses can recruit the most qualified workers based on previously unmeasured data, thus mitigating subconscious prejudices. We've also learned that artificial intelligence will not steal jobs; it will take over functions that allow HR workers to play to their strengths.

Ultimately, artificial intelligence helps HR departments shift from administrative tasks to strategic roles. It makes seemingly unmeasurable data—like an individual's propensity for generosity and innovation or trends that catalyze an engaged team—into measurable milestones, giving your small business tangible goals to become a better company.

Chapter 10

AI + Data Analysis and Decision-Making

Artificial intelligence makes data accessible for everyone, particularly people in business. Data processing and analytics have depended on algorithms for decades, but artificial technology makes formerly daunting equations digestible for the layperson. With AI in your corner, you can obtain complex and powerful data insights for your business needs without requiring a degree in data science. As you've uncovered through specific examples in this book, artificial intelligence can overhaul your business decision-making process in a very positive way. At unrivaled speeds, AI can review gigantic amounts of data and, importantly, uncover trends that might be unnoticed by the human eye. Your business will be poised to make better decisions in virtually every facet of your organization.

This chapter is a call to action. With artificial intelligence, you can analyze data until the cows come home. It's up to you to go to the next level and use AI's vast data processing capabilities to make sound, strategic choices for your business.

HOW TO USE AI FOR STRATEGIC DECISION-MAKING

I'll be the first to admit that I am not a typical "data" person. I don't love spreadsheets, calculations, or analysis. Now thanks to artificial intelligence, that's perfectly okay. I have found many accessible tools to help me understand the conclusions of analysis without having to wield algo-rithms myself. I do, however, have a client who is very much a data person, and I will use her business to illustrate the power of artificial intelligence.

AI in Practice

Dana Benjamin is the founder of Back of the Napkin Consulting, a strategic consultancy firm in the Boston area that helps mission-driven organizations use data to achieve a positive impact. A significant por-tion of Back of the Napkin's clientele includes Boys & Girls Clubs across America.

Here's a quick overview if you aren't familiar with how Boys & Girls Clubs operate: Boys & Girls Clubs are nonprofit organizations commit-ted to providing youth safe places to grow and learn, especially outside school hours. Generally, the Boys & Girls Club locations will have pro-grams critical to youth development, such as health, leadership, educa-tion, art, and physical fitness. Boys & Girls Clubs of America (BGCA) is the umbrella organization at a national level, supporting local clubs with training, advocacy efforts, and program development. The local clubs function independently but follow the recommendations and guidelines determined by BGCA.

At a local level, there is usually a local board of directors for each Boys & Girls Club. Those directors oversee and lead strategic planning, fundraising, and overall operations. (For reference, Dana's clients are usu-ally these local boards.) Each local organization receives funding from the government—federal and state grants—and local grants focused on educational programs and youth development. These local boards can also receive donations from individuals and corporations, and some may charge a low membership fee for members. Galas and fundraising events can also be a cornerstone of funding for these local chapters.

Here's where Back of the Napkin comes in: Their firm clarifies data for local chapters, so every raised dollar maximizes their mission and efforts. Dana's job has many layers, some of which I suspect will be rele-vant to your organization:

- Identifying trends where money is generated.
- Tracking new members, returning members, and attrition rates.
- Analyzing the demographics of members.
- Tailoring programs based on member demographics.
- Measuring participation rates in different programs.
- Evaluating program popularity.
- Adjusting program offerings based on demands.
- Tracking performance improvements in members (like school attendance or grades).
- Collecting self-reported assessments from members on personal development.
- Recording the philanthropic hours of community volunteers.
- Identifying trends among community volunteers.
- Analyzing patterns in fundraising, like events, campaigns, and grant funding.
- Tracking donor retention rate.
- Analyzing average donation amounts in comparison to economic and market trends.
- Identifying cost-saving opportunities.
- Monitoring expenses and revenues.
- Understanding volunteer and staff satisfaction ratings.
- Tracking use of facilities and equipment.
- And more.

Dana and her team have been data experts out of necessity. Projects can be long, sometimes requiring months of data organization and systems updates to improve on how data is collected. Once the data is obtained and organized, it has to be interpreted by a human, who then turns it into a strategy. With artificial intelligence, Dana and her team can hand off three critical steps (organization, collection, and interpretation) to focus on making strategic decisions that generate impact.

PREFERRED PLATFORMS FOR ANALYSIS

Here are some tools you could use to help with data collection, insights, and analysis:

- **Sisense.** Sisense merges data visualization, data insights, and predictive analytics to help businesses make data-driven decisions. Trusted by Skullcandy, Nasdaq, Verizon, and more, Sisense's AI insights and analytical engine help users make better business choices with easy-to-understand visuals.
- **Looker.** Looker's artificial intelligence technology helps users explore, analyze, and share real-time business analytics. It integrates seamlessly with Google Cloud and features customized dashboards and reporting capabilities for data presentation.
- **People.ai.** An AI-powered revenue intelligence platform, People .ai provides in-depth data collection, analysis, and insights particularly geared for sales, marketing, and customer service teams. It automatically captures customer data without manual entry (including across emails and calls), and the tool also provides personalized data-driven suggestions to coach sales representatives.
- **Qualtrics XM.** This tool is a leader in measuring business verticals related to customers, employees, products, and brands. Its built-in artificial intelligence and machine learning analyze data to provide recommended improvements in customer and employee satisfaction while also forecasting behaviors and preferences.
- **Salesforce Nonprofit Cloud.** Salesforce Nonprofit Cloud brings artificial intelligence insight for the management and analysis of fundraising, grants, donors, volunteers, and programs. It seamlessly integrates with other programs in the Salesforce suite as well.

MANAGING BIG DATA WITH ARTIFICIAL INTELLIGENCE

"Big data" refers to incredibly large and complex datasets that traditional methods—such as manual analysis, basic statistical tools, or nonspecialized software—just can't handle. These massive amounts of information can come from various sources, including social media, sensors, and transaction records. Navigating big data can be complex, especially for a small business, but here is the good news—artificial intelligence can carry the management of these vast datasets. By harnessing AI, you can analyze big data to uncover hidden patterns, trends, and insights that can significantly enhance your decision-making and strategic planning. In today's digital age, you're flooded with information, including:

- Customer transaction details, like purchases, returns, exchanges, and associated behaviors while shopping.
- Social media data, ranging all the way from post-level analytics to page-level analytics to individual conversations with users.
- Website analytics, like page views, bounce rates, time on site, and the overall user journey on your site.
- Sensor data, which comes from devices like smart home products, wearable gadgets, vehicle telematics, and sensors on manufacturing equipment.
- Geolocation data, where you get information on the physical location of your customers and assets.
- Machine logs, which is data generated by networks, servers, and computer systems.
- Email and communication, including customer service conversations, email exchanges between employees, and live chat records.
- Healthcare records, like patient records, treatment histories, clinical trial data, and research study conclusions.
- Market research, such as customer surveys, feedback forms, and focus groups.

Your business likely has access to much of this data, which if analyzed and interpreted correctly can be invaluable for your business. With artificial intelligence, you can rapidly review this information to make better decisions that move your business forward. Instead of staying in a purgatory of "analysis paralysis," AI can be a trampoline for businesses that want to act.

Use the insights of a generative AI tool such as ChatGPT to understand the big data your business collects and determine opportunities to streamline. Here's an example you can use to inspire your exploration:

 I am a social worker who does in-person and virtual therapy sessions for my independent practice. I want to leverage artificial intelligence to manage and analyze my data. Can you please brainstorm the types of big data my business collects?

 Certainly! In your practice as a social worker offering in-person and virtual therapy sessions, you're likely to collect a variety of data that can be enhanced and understood better with the aid of artificial intelligence. Leveraging AI can help in managing, analyzing, and utilizing this data to improve your services, tailor interventions, and enhance patient outcomes. Here's a brainstorm of the types of big data your business may collect:

- **Patient Demographics**
    a. Age, gender, and ethnicity: Basic demographic information can help tailor therapy approaches based on population-specific trends.
    b. Socioeconomic status: May influence the type of support and resources a patient might need.

- **Clinical Data**
    a. Symptom records and severity: Tracking symptom changes over time can help in measuring treatment effectiveness.
    b. Diagnosis information: Knowing the distribution of various conditions treated can help in resource planning and specialization.

c. Treatment plans and outcomes: Detailed records can aid in analyzing what treatment strategies work best for different conditions or demographics.

- **Session Notes and Observations**
  - a. Text data from therapy sessions: Through natural language processing, AI can analyze session transcripts for themes, progress indicators, and more.
  - b. Nonverbal cues in virtual sessions: Video analytics can potentially evaluate nonverbal cues like facial expressions or body language.

- **Interaction Data**
  - a. Appointment scheduling and frequency: Patterns in scheduling can inform about patient engagement and the effectiveness of therapy schedules.
  - b. Communication outside sessions: Emails, texts, or phone call logs can provide insights into patient needs and engagement levels.

- **Feedback and Satisfaction Data**
  - a. Patient feedback forms: Analyzing feedback can highlight areas for improvement and patient satisfaction levels.
  - b. Outcome measures: Pre- and posttreatment assessments can be analyzed to measure therapeutic effectiveness over large datasets.

- **Digital Usage Data**
  - a. Website and app usage patterns: Understanding how patients interact with your digital tools can help improve user experience and accessibility.
  - b. Virtual session analytics: Data on session duration, technical issues, and platform preferences can inform technical improvements and training needs.

• **Health and Lifestyle Data**
  a. Wearable device data: If patients agree to share, data from fitness trackers or health apps can provide insights into physical activity, sleep patterns, and more, which are relevant to mental health.

 • **External Sources**
  a. Social determinants of health: Information from public databases or partnerships with other organizations can provide context on external factors affecting your patients.

Leveraging AI in analyzing these data types can help you identify trends, predict outcomes, tailor treatments, and improve overall service delivery. Importantly, ethical considerations, data privacy, and security should be paramount in any data handling and analysis to protect patient confidentiality and comply with regulations like HIPAA.

Make Smarter Operational Decisions

What AI can do: Aggregate and analyze data to give you objective information on which to base decisions.

Recommended AI tools for this task: Microsoft Azure AI, Oracle AI, Alteryx, DataRobot

Data you might need on hand: Operational data, financial data, customer data, supply chain data, market data, employee performance data

Operations and logistics might seem like "mechanical" parts of businesses, but immense strategy is required to make logistic processes successful. Strategic decision-making in this field helps you maximize efficiencies across operations, improve customer satisfaction, mitigate risk, increase your edge over competitors, bounce back during setbacks, allocate resources optimally, and create a business that's set up for long-term success.

Without strategic thinking, your operations are akin to being a hamster on a wheel: You might be active, but you're directionless. To continue growing as a business, you need to move closer to your goal destination. Artificial intelligence helps you make better strategic decisions by synthesizing and articulating data. Whether you're a team of one or a team of thirty, AI's deep insights can help you accept the cold, hard facts of your company—so you can focus on improving faster.

Preferred Platforms for Decision-Making

Here are a few tools to try when you want help with strategic decision-making:

- **Microsoft Azure AI.** Microsoft Azure AI is a suite of AI tools focused on helping businesses build their own AI solutions. These tools can be leveraged to create artificial intelligence solutions that are completely customized for your business, such as predicting optimal delivery times, comparing customer service data to deliveries, and more.

- **Oracle AI.** With a comprehensive suite of AI tools, Oracle AI can be used to help a variety of business functions, including operations and logistics as well as HR, finance, and customer experience. It can be used for automation processes, predictive analytics, and operational efficiencies.

- **Alteryx.** Alteryx's AI-fueled platform combines generative and conversational AI, data science, reporting, and automation to help businesses make data-driven decisions for their company. Trusted by over eight thousand companies globally, Alteryx can help multiple teams and departments access data and benefit from its predictive analytics capabilities.

- **DataRobot.** Think of DataRobot as a brilliant data assistant that can drive business growth. Its automated machine-learning technology helps users quickly develop and launch models for their business needs, such as integrating with your IT infrastructure, creating predictive analytics models, and more. The tool makes complex data science accessible, and it can be used for almost all areas of operations and logistics.

- **Microsoft Power BI.** Microsoft Power BI is an AI-powered data visualization tool that enables small businesses to convert complex datasets into easy-to-understand visual formats like charts, graphs, and dashboards. Power BI's AI features can automatically analyze data trends, highlight key insights, and suggest the most effective ways to visualize the data, helping users make data-driven decisions quickly and confidently.

Clean Up Your Data

What AI can do: Identify and potentially correct errors in your data.

Recommended AI tools for this task: Alteryx Designer Cloud

Data you might need on hand: Raw data, data accuracy information, error logs and reports

Yes, it's important to collect data, but with so much data at your fingertips, it's also essential to know what data is *correct*. Luckily, artificial intelligence adds precision and speed to a previously arduous task, zipping through data to identify what is necessary for your goals or records and eliminating errors and inconsistencies.

Let's consider how AI could help the world of healthcare, where accurate data can sometimes be a matter of life or death. A single mistake or data error in a patient's record could result in misdiagnoses, ineffective treatments, and more. And if a data error occurs in a research study? The consequences would be exponential.

With an artificial intelligence tool like Alteryx Designer Cloud (formerly Trifacta), you don't need to hire a data specialist to comb through data. Alteryx could automate the process of identifying and correcting any data errors found in patient records and research datasets. Doctors could be confident knowing they're making patient recommendations based on factually correct data, and countless hours would be saved in data review.

Alteryx also works outside of healthcare. The artificial intelligence tool is beneficial for cleaning data in many industries, including retail, financial services, manufacturing, government, telecommunications, energy and utilities, and transportation.

Merge Data from Multiple Sources

What AI can do: Combine and assess data procured from multiple sources.

Recommended AI tools for this task: Talend

Data you might need on hand: Source data, data schemas, connection details, metadata, integration requirements, security and compliance information

Previous chapters have reviewed the challenges and issues of siloed data sources—and how artificial intelligence can act as your business's glue by connecting multiple data storage areas. As a business, you need to ensure a complete picture of the data you're handling, and having data in separate pools isn't helpful for anyone.

Without artificial intelligence's help, you might need to hire a specialist to overhaul your data collection systems, complete with analysis, mapped collection workflow, and tool analysis, and then rebuild your entire collection framework. Artificial intelligence lets businesses skip this step by assessing and merging data from multiple sources, with the added value of analyzing the data.

To envision this in action, picture a retail chain. They collect customer data through online sales, in-store purchases, social media interactions, and customer service communications in their store and online. Each of these verticals has its own data, housed completely separately. Any time the retail chain wants to understand customer behavior, they must dedicate days to creating a patchwork of data from these different sources. By the time the data is collected, the team is so exhausted that the analysis is high-level, and no action is taken because the days of data sorting distract from other daily responsibilities.

If this retail chain used a tool like Talend, their data would constantly be integrated and managed. The cloud-based software combines data from multiple sources, even for in-person versus online transactions. Once the data is integrated, the retail chain would have a holistic view of its customer data, which would make it easier to create customer segments for personalized marketing campaigns and for simply understanding customers from a more informed perspective. Talend's artificial intelligence automates data integration, ensuring that businesses always have up-to-date information.

Analyze Textual Data

What AI can do: "Read" and analyze text-based data.

Recommended AI tools for this task: Qualtrics Social Connect

Data you might need on hand: Text data sources (like written documents, emails, messages, and even speech transcripts), metadata, data formats, analysis criteria

Textual data, found in writing, documents, emails, messages, and even speech, can be critical for uncovering consumer insights. This type of data can disclose how your customers *really* feel about your product, but it can also shed light on other customer problems that could be a potential product or offering for your small business. Artificial intelligence can synthesize textual data from ample sources, formulating a clear picture of your consumer demands, potential behavioral shifts, and product feedback.

If a consumer goods company wants to create a new product, employing artificial intelligence can help the cause dramatically. By having an AI tool like Qualtrics Connect, formerly known as Clarabridge, sift through public conversations, reviews, and feedback, along with their own internal textual data, the small business will have a factual and comprehensive summary of competing solutions by competitors, existing sentiments about their brand, pressing pain points of customers, and more. Armed with AI's in-depth data—*textual* data—analysis, company stakeholders can confidently make decisions, knowing that cold, hard facts are on their side.

Harness the Power of Spreadsheets

What AI can do: Enhance spreadsheet functionality by automating data analysis and generating insights.

Recommended AI tools for this task: Excel, Google Sheets, BigQuery

Data you might need on hand: Spreadsheet data, data schemas, connection details, data quality metrics, analysis criteria, security and compliance information

If you're not ready to loosen your grip on Microsoft Excel, fear not. Artificial intelligence add-ons can augment your spreadsheet experience until you're ready to take the leap to other advanced applications. You don't need to manually plunk away at data or look up a certain formula in a cell anymore. AI is, more than likely, already part of your spreadsheet software, and you'll immediately reap the benefits.

If you're an Excel user on Microsoft 365, you'll be pleased to know that artificial intelligence can analyze your data and synthesize conclusions right within the program. Just use Excel's "Analyze Data" feature and sit back while its artificial intelligence technology articulates your data's trends and patterns within seconds. Predictive analytics are also very much part of Excel, and the AI can forecast trends based on the data that's already in your spreadsheet. Budgeting, forecasting sales, managing inventory—it's all immediately easier.

Excel also features natural language processing capabilities. As part of its "Tell Me" feature that's right within the software, you can use everyday colloquial language to ask questions or make commands like, "Show me how to remove duplicates," "What formula do I use to calculate a loan payment?" and "How can I automate repetitive tasks with macro formulas?" After you make your request, the AI's natural language processing gets to work, quickly providing you with the necessary information.

If you're bogged down by a spreadsheet cleanup project, still no stress there: Excel's "Data Types" artificial intelligence, available in Microsoft 365, can identify and update data. For example, if a travel agency owner wants to make a spreadsheet with information about countries, like currency and language, the "Data Types" feature would pull data directly from the Internet to populate the empty columns with correct information.

More of a Google Sheets fan? Artificial intelligence is also part of the Google browser–based software. The next time you're in Google Sheets, pay attention to any data that's automatically filled in—because it's artificial intelligence at work. The "Data Cleanup" feature can address any data inconsistencies (like formatting errors or duplicates) to help you prepare your data. If you're working with a sheet that has terabytes' worth of data, Google has a "Connected Sheets" feature where you can use AI technology from BigQuery (Google's multicloud data warehouse) within your sheet. In this scenario, you'll experience BigQuery's machine learning and advanced data analysis capabilities—without needing any experience with SQL.

Convert Data to Visual Formats

What AI can do: Assess various pieces of data and determine the clearest way to show that data visually (e.g., charts, graphs, word clouds, etc.).

Recommended AI tools for this task: Microsoft Power BI

Data you might need on hand: Any data you'd like to show in an easy-to-digest format

Artificial intelligence's unparalleled data analysis abilities can be a double-edged sword for leaders within small businesses. On the one hand, there are seemingly endless ways to slice and dice data and then receive a sophisticated interpretation of the most minor of data points from AI. But on the other hand, the volume of these insights can be overwhelming. At some point, analyses and recommendations become moot without action. For this reason, *visualizing* data with AI-driven tools can help inspire business decision-making. When you can see the data, often the choice can feel like it's already made for you.

AI in Practice

My client Mark Maynard might greatly benefit from visualizing data to help his clients make strategic and informed decisions fast. Mark, a seasoned consultant and executive coach, has over three decades of experience conceptualizing, building, managing, and leading businesses, particularly within the hospitality sector. Mark's clients come from a wide range of industries, but they all share a need for guidance in taking their business from status quo to excellent, whether it's their operations or leadership.

Let's say Mark has been hired to advise the CEO of a farm-to-table restaurant chain. Despite an avid and frequent customer base and high sales volume, the chain's profit margins have wildly fluctuated. The CEO has hired Mark to figure out what's going on and determine a fix.

Mark, based on his experience with executives, thinks visuals will be the best way to present his discoveries and recommendations. He uses Microsoft Power BI, an AI-powered visualization tool, to share the following in a meeting with the CEO:

- A visualization of the business's profit and loss statements from the past three years. The artificial intelligence depicts any drastic fluctuations in food costs and other seasonality impacts, making it easy to see when these strains are happening with specificity.
- A visual analysis of food cost management, where artificial intelligence identifies ingredients with volatile pricing and cross-references to the price of menu items. This way, Mark and the CEO can see any dishes with an inconsistent or unfavorable cost-to-profit ratio.
- A chart of operational expenses, such as staff, utilities, and maintenance costs. Mark has the AI connect these costs with peak dining times, showing overstaffing in slow periods and higher-than-desired utility costs outside peak hours.
- A comprehensive menu analysis that pinpoints bestselling and underperforming dishes. The artificial intelligence thoroughly analyzes each item's profitability while also considering ingredient cost fluctuation.

As you can imagine, seeing highly simplified and interactive charts of these observations would be much easier to digest. Once visualized, the CEO might be more inspired to act on Mark's recommendations, which include:

- Removing underperforming dishes with an undesirable profit margin.
- Adjusting popular menu prices quarterly based on volatile ingredients' seasonal costs.
- Negotiating with suppliers or exploring alternative items for the high-cost ingredients.
- Revising the staffing model during slow dining times.
- Implementing energy-saving protocols during off-peak hours.
- Promoting high-profit dishes in a menu redesign.

With the help of artificial intelligence's data visualization capabilities, data is presented in a way that's digestible and actionable. Recommendations are trusted, and decision-making becomes easier—all because AI's insights can fuel meaningful business discussions.

EXPERIENCE ENLIGHTENED DECISION-MAKING WITH ARTIFICIAL INTELLIGENCE

Artificial intelligence's data analysis has revolutionized the ways that small businesses can make important business decisions. From cleaning erroneous data with Alteryx to creating visuals with Microsoft Power BI, businesses of all sizes—even businesses of one—can now access data in a deeper and more insightful way. You don't need to have a data scientist on your team to obtain strategic advantages through insights; artificial intelligence's elite tools can do this for you.

Here's my prediction: We're in the nascent stages of artificial intelligence being a decision-making tool for small businesses. The sooner you adopt this technology into your business, the sooner you can *adapt* when this technology inevitably evolves.

Chapter 11

AI + Security and Legal Compliance

R unning a small business comes with its fair share of challenges, from keeping customers happy to achieving quarterly goals. But those tasks can pale in comparison to the stress of a security or legal issue, especially if you don't have the funds for proper legal or cybersecurity guidance.

Even if you're a business of one, small businesses are no strangers to security and legal issues. If your website or emails are hacked, you must worry about the protection of sensitive data. If you aren't up-to-date on legal regulations, you can risk a lawsuit or hefty fine. If you don't have a system for managing your contracts, your business might be at risk if something goes awry.

Thankfully, artificial intelligence can act as your preliminary counsel, on-demand guide, and first line of defense with all things security and legal. This chapter will detail how you can protect your business in those critical areas so, if something does come up, you'll know exactly what steps to take next.

AI'S TRANSFORMATION OF RISK MANAGEMENT

As a small business owner myself, I recognize how challenging it can be to stay up-to-date with the latest legal developments and security measures necessary to protect my customers and my business. I run a business of one with trusted contractors, and I don't have endless funds to throw at lawyers and cybersecurity experts. For most small businesses, you're either big enough to hire the necessary experts regularly without consequence or small and vulnerable.

Over the years, there have been some developments in the risk management world to help fill this gap that small businesses occupy. There's standard antivirus software—you might recognize names like McAfee or Norton—that can protect against known malware and viruses, and some modern solutions incorporate behavioral analysis and machine learning to handle new or evolving cybersecurity threats. There are firewalls—Cisco and Fortinet—but many now include next-generation features to better adapt to evolving technology threats. From a legal standpoint, you can pull a standard contract off the Internet and use DocuSign, but this won't highlight potential issues or suggested optimizations for your contracts.

With artificial intelligence, small businesses don't have to feel as isolated in risk management. AI systems are adaptable, continuously learning from new data, and with this comes the ability to instantly evolve—to security threats and legal changes. Artificial intelligence's predictive powers also come into play in your business's online safety, equipping you with proactive insights into what current risks and vulnerabilities might become future problems. Small businesses can also benefit from AI's personalization capabilities, where you'll receive legal and security recommendations unique to your specific business needs.

The previously mentioned risk management software is better than nothing, but with reasonably priced artificial intelligence tools, artificial intelligence provides a dynamic and comprehensive risk management reservoir for your business's tool kit. Not every small business is comfortable with the digital landscape, and artificial intelligence brings approachable and sophisticated legal and security solutions that were previously unavailable. The upcoming sections will help you learn how to protect yourself from risks while also gaining a competitive edge that fortifies you.

PREFERRED PLATFORMS FOR LEGAL TASKS

Here are some tools to help with your legal and contractual documents:

- **Icertis.** This contract management tool is an AI-powered cloud-based solution that can handle every aspect of your business contracts from start to finish. The AI's analytics provide detailed analyses of your contracts so you understand obligations and potential risks. It also ensures your contracts match any internal company policies to mitigate risk.

- **ContractPodAi.** Bringing automation to the contracting process, ContractPodAi specializes in drafting, negotiating, approving, and analyzing contracts with the power of artificial intelligence. The tool has a library of templates and clauses to insert into your agreements and a repository that makes it easy to search for past contracts.

- **Kira Systems.** Kira's artificial intelligence utilizes machine learning for contracts and due diligence. The AI was trained by experienced subject matter experts, including lawyers and accountants from KPMG, PayPal, and Bank of Montreal, so it can contextualize contract information and answer any questions you have before signing.

- **ROSS Intelligence.** If you're a lawyer within a small business, ROSS Intelligence might be of interest. The artificial intelligence tool can conduct fast and in-depth legal research, analyze documents (including arguments), and help you identify cases that have been overturned or criticized.

- **DoNotPay.** Known as "the world's first robot lawyer," DoNotPay is an artificial intelligence tool that handles legal manual tasks. From fighting bank fees to ordering marriage certificates to appealing parking tickets, DoNotPay helps consumers exercise rights through customized legal documents, automated legal assistance, and accessibility to complex legal procedures.

- **LawDroid.** LawDroid is marketed as a chatbot for attorneys and litigation professionals, but it's also an adequate solution for people who have basic legal questions but aren't ready to consult a lawyer. LawDroid's Copilot, a built-in artificial intelligence feature, is a legal assistant that can help you research legal issues, draft letters, and summarize documents.

WHAT ARE YOUR BUSINESS'S IMMEDIATE THREATS?

Before you get into this chapter any further, take some time and think about your business's immediate threats—the worst-case scenarios that keep you up at night. This will give you a good starting point of where to start with adding AI to your risk management process.

When Was the Last Time a Lawyer Updated Your Legal Documents or Contracts?

People often don't think of how important legal documents are until something goes wrong. In all industries, laws and regulations frequently change. If your business isn't up-to-date, this lack of compliance could result in penalties or, worse, legal action. Legal documents can be your shield against litigation, saving you thousands in legal fees, and they can also be an opportunity to establish and maintain trust with your clients, partners, customers, and team.

An AI-powered tool like Superlegal is, in my eyes, the next closest thing to having a lawyer at your disposal. The tool understands the contractual context of your business, and its patented AI technology redlines contracts and negotiates with the counterparty. The platform provides the precision of an attorney without the cost, with a measured 94% accuracy.

How Would You Know If Someone Hacked Into Your Business Systems?

Unlike the blatant "Oh no! We've been hacked!" lines you might see in a movie or TV show, unauthorized systems access can be stealthy. It could be months before you know your business has been compromised, and without the right tools, you might not know until it's too late.

Your business systems are critical for your business's infrastructure. You probably have vulnerable customer information stored in your payment processors (like mailing addresses and emails), confidential correspondence, financial information about your business, and more. A hacker can steal this information and, in some cases, upend your entire business. Some will even hold that data at ransom! Cybersecurity is no laughing matter, and it's imperative to know about your systems' vulnerabilities and compromises.

Artificial intelligence provides awareness and protection against weak spots and unauthorized access to your business's cybersecurity. SentinelOne is an AI-powered security platform that protects your assets, cloud, and identities from hackers. The tool is trusted by Aston Martin, Norwegian Airlines, Samsung, Canva, and Q2 and gives you unparalleled visibility into your network. Its artificial intelligence monitors your systems 24/7, and its advanced algorithms uncover vulnerabilities that humans might miss. You'll be alerted about potential breaches in detail, including insights into the threat, and it can isolate any compromised systems to prevent the breach from spreading.

If Private Customer Information Was Accidentally Leaked from Your Business, What's Your Plan?

Data protection is a legal must today. Europe's GDPR sets an international standard that now many other countries are following, which requires businesses to add extra precautions for customers' personal information, including notifying if there's a security breach. These privacy guides aren't just suggestions—they're *laws*, and you, as a small business, have a legal requirement to comply.

Aside from the legal aspects of data protection, it's also essential from a trust standpoint. If your customers choose to do business with you, they also trust you'll have the necessary safeguards to protect their information from hackers and leaks. As Warren Buffett once said, "It takes twenty years to build a reputation and 5 minutes to ruin it," and, with AI technology, data leaks don't have to be a risk of your company's downfall.

Darktrace is an AI-powered cybersecurity tool that monitors your systems from the inside. Darktrace monitors your network to understand "status quo" activity, such as user behaviors, device interactions, and the general flow of data. With its rapid data analysis abilities, Darktrace can understand what a typical day in your organization looks like from a technological perspective. Once the baseline has been established, Darktrace constantly monitors and measures network activities in comparison to what's normal. If there's a suspicious pattern or an unusual attempt to export data (like customer information), it would flag the potential security breach and implement actions to halt the threat that very second. You'll also get a detailed investigation of the situation's forensics, such as time stamps and location of affected systems, allowing you to take steps that protect your business in the future.

You don't need deep pockets to have state-of-the-art cybersecurity and legal counsel. With artificial intelligence, you can have detailed contract reviews and negotiations, external shields from hackers, and ever-constant monitoring of your internal systems.

Preferred Platforms for Security

Here are some tools that can help you monitor your security and protect your customer's information:

- **Crowdstrike Falcon.** With sophisticated artificial intelligence technology, Crowdstrike Falcon combines machine learning and behavioral analytics into an all-in-one cybersecurity protection tool. The tool possesses both endpoint protection (EPP) and endpoint detection and response (EDR) for a comprehensive solution.
- **Palo Alto Networks Cortex.** Palo Alto Networks Cortex uses artificial intelligence to monitor and alert about any hackers. It's the virtual equivalent of having security cameras on your virtual property, where alarms will sound if anyone tries to break in. Its AI also tracks data of any hacking attempts and then synthesizes the records to suggest fixes for better security.

- **Cybereason.** Cybereason is like a digital guard dog attacking when anyone tries to break into your small business's network or devices. It can identify and mitigate malware, ransomware, and other threats typically made on network endpoints like laptops, desktops, and mobile devices.
- **BetterCloud.** BetterCloud is a SaaS operations management platform that helps you automate IT tasks and processes, like onboarding and offboarding employees. The tool helps you enforce security policies across cloud applications, detects unauthorized data access, and includes precautions against data breaches.
- **Onfido.** Onfido uses AI to verify identities by analyzing government-issued documents and biometric data, such as facial recognition. Its machine learning algorithms continually adapt to detect and prevent fraud, making it a powerful tool for small businesses seeking scalable protection against identity theft and fraudulent transactions.
- **Socure.** Socure leverages AI and predictive analytics to assess identity risks in real time, analyzing data like identity documents and device fingerprints. Its high accuracy in fraud detection helps small businesses secure their online transactions, minimizing risks without compromising customer experience.

PROTECTING YOUR CONTENT FROM ARTIFICIAL INTELLIGENCE

AI's machine learning is a superpower and, depending on who you are, a weapon. While I am (obviously) pro artificial intelligence, I'm also conscious that AI knowledge is obtained by scraping large datasets, including what's found on the Internet. Every time you post something online, you're sharing intellectual property, and that intellectual property could be scraped by artificial intelligence. Your content can be sponged up and potentially become a reference point in how AI writes, creates images, and generates ideas for other users in similar industries. This isn't necessarily a "bad" thing, but if you're worried about your content (like blog posts, product descriptions, or images) being repurposed by AI crawlers, I recommend potentially blocking these crawlers from accessing your site.

Many of my clients, as well as my own website, use Squarespace, which is why I'm highlighting its unique approach to protecting content from AI crawlers. Squarespace websites allow users to proactively protect content from AI crawlers. As I learned from my friend Becca Harpain, a recognized Squarespace CSS expert, the platform offers a straightforward option to block AI from scraping website content. By navigating to the "Settings" menu and selecting "Crawlers," users can disable access for artificial intelligence crawlers across their entire site, not just on a page-by-page basis. However, it's important to note that any data already scraped by AI cannot be removed, and blocking Google AI bots requires blocking all Google bots, including those that gather information for organic search engine results.

Additionally, both WordPress and Wix offer similar features to prevent AI bots from scraping website content. WordPress has a plugin that can block a wide range of AI crawlers, modifying the robots.txt file and adding specific meta tags to discourage AI use of your content. Wix, while not as focused on AI crawler blocking, provides robust customization options and tools that help manage site visibility and interaction with bots.

These features are particularly significant for content creators who wish to safeguard their intellectual property and ensure that their content remains exclusively for human consumption. Squarespace's initiative to empower users with this level of control is a commendable step toward protecting privacy in the digital age, making it a platform that respects the intentions of its users regarding the visibility and use of their content by AI technologies.

Verify People's Identities

What AI can do: Confirm an individual's identity to protect your business from fraud.

Recommended AI tools for this task: Onfido, Secure

Data you might need on hand: Identity documents, biometric data, transactional data

If you operate a small business with transactions involving large sums of money, such as fine jewelry, art, or cars, you've likely considered or have opened an online store to complement your in-person experience. With an online store, you can reach a wider and potentially global customer base, and it doesn't require permanent staffing shifts like with a brick-and-mortar location. However, without adequate identity verification measures, your online business could experience significant risks, such as:

- Financial losses from fraudulent transactions, like cost of the goods and shipping.
- Legal or regulatory penalties from lack of compliance.
- Erosion of customer trust if fraud or identity theft is part of the transaction.
- Lost time and operational revenues from the aftermath of a fraudulent transaction.
- Higher processing fees or termination of services from banks and payment processors.

Thankfully, there are plenty of artificial intelligence solutions to help safeguard your business, goods, and reputation against these deceptive scammers. Onfido and Socure are popular AI solutions because of their comprehensive verification offerings, which include document verification, biometric analysis, and fraud detection. With artificial intelligence leading your company's verification efforts, you can rely on data processing and machine learning to confirm an individual's identity. For document verification, artificial intelligence can detect tampering or fraud in government-issued ID documents; this would be essential if you're selling a car and need to confirm a driver's license. For facial recognition, artificial intelligence can compare a live selfie to the ID's image, and its biometric analysis can detect anomalies.

The best part of these AI-powered verification tools? Machine-learning capabilities ensure that artificial intelligence is constantly learning. With every transaction, your tool will become even more finely tuned, offering a proficient precaution that can sign off on large transactions while you sleep. If you're intimidated by how to set up the technology, don't worry. Once you've selected an AI-powered verification tool, you can quite effortlessly integrate the tool with your online store, generally on the checkout or account creation pages. Most artificial intelligence tools integrate through an API, ensuring the artificial intelligence is constantly synced with any transactions on your site.

Offer Basic Legal Guidance and Services

What AI can do: Serve as a quick resource for legal questions.

Recommended AI tools for this task: DoNotPay, LawDroid

Data you might need on hand: Legal questions and scenarios, relevant documents, case history

Wish you could have a legal expert in your pocket, just in case? Well, with artificial intelligence, you can. Legal chatbots, powered by artificial intelligence, offer on-the-spot legal guidance for common legal questions. The tools are becoming increasingly used by law firms (throwback to our customer service chapter!) as an instantaneous resource for clients, but you don't need to be a law firm to benefit from this incredible technology.

One of my favorite client projects is Planespoken, a pilot-founded company that provides specialized risk management workshops. Founded by Marcus Eyers, Planespoken shares the rigorous risk management techniques of pilots with organizations across all industries, inspiring them to take action on vulnerabilities in their establishment.

Imagine Marcus is giving a presentation to a mining company, an industry he's not very familiar with. In advance of his workshop, Marcus could leverage artificial intelligence to provide customized solutions to the company's specific risk management issues. Using a generative AI tool, he could get text to generate a survey that's distributed to all attendees.

AI in Action

Try a variation of this prompt:

I am the founder of Planespoken, a pilot-founded company that shares the risk management techniques of pilots with companies of all industries. I am giving a workshop to a mining company and want to better understand their vulnerabilities from a legal, operational, and cybersecurity standpoint. Please generate a survey of twenty questions that can help me get as much information as possible. For reference, I plan on running their information through a legal chatbot after to understand certain legalities, so please keep this in mind when creating your questionnaire items.

Creating a comprehensive survey for a mining company involves considering various aspects of their operations, legal obligations, and cybersecurity posture. Given your aim to apply pilot risk management techniques and further analyze the legal nuances with a legal chatbot, the questions should be designed to elicit detailed responses that cover these areas thoroughly. Here's a survey of twenty questions that can help you gather the necessary information:

Legal Vulnerabilities:

1. **Regulatory Compliance:** Can you detail your company's efforts to comply with local, national, and international mining regulations?

2. **Environmental Regulations:** How does your company ensure compliance with environmental regulations and manage the risk of environmental lawsuits?

3. **Labor Laws:** Could you describe your adherence to labor laws and regulations, including worker safety and fair compensation practices?

4. **Land Rights and Usage:** How does your company address land rights and usage disputes, including operations on indigenous lands or protected areas?

5. **Litigation History:** Has your company faced any legal actions or litigations related to your mining operations? If so, please provide details.

Operational Vulnerabilities:

1. **Health and Safety Protocols:** What health and safety protocols are in place to protect workers from occupational hazards specific to mining?

2. **Emergency Response:** Can you outline your emergency response plan for incidents like mine collapse, chemical spills, or other accidents?

3. **Supply Chain Management:** How does your company manage supply chain risks, especially in terms of critical equipment and materials procurement?

4. **Operational Efficiency:** What measures are in place to monitor and improve the operational efficiency and productivity of your mining operations?

5. **Environmental Impact and Sustainability:** How do you assess and mitigate the environmental impact of your mining operations, including water usage and waste management?

Cybersecurity Vulnerabilities:

1. **Cybersecurity Measures:** What cybersecurity measures are in place to protect against external and internal threats?

2. **Data Protection:** How does your company ensure the protection of sensitive data, including employee information and proprietary data?

3. **Incident Response Plan:** Does your company have a cyber incident response plan? If so, how often is it tested or updated?

4. **Third-Party Vendors:** How do you assess and monitor the cybersecurity practices of third-party vendors and partners?

5. **Employee Training:** What kind of cybersecurity training do employees receive, and how frequently is it conducted?

General Questions:

1. **Risk Management Practices:** How does your company identify, assess, and manage risks associated with your mining operations?

2. **Innovation and Technology:** Are there any innovative technologies or practices your company is exploring to enhance safety, efficiency, or sustainability?

3. **Stakeholder Engagement:** How does your company engage with stakeholders, including local communities, governments, and environmental groups?

4. **Future Challenges:** What are the most significant challenges your company anticipates in the coming years, and how are you preparing to address them?

5. **Legal Compliance:** How does your company stay updated and ensure compliance with evolving legal standards and regulations in the mining industry?

This survey aims to provide a comprehensive overview of the company's legal, operational, and cybersecurity vulnerabilities. The responses should offer valuable insights for applying risk management techniques and understanding legal considerations through your subsequent analysis with a legal chatbot.

(By the way, feel free to answer these questions for your own company as a way to better understand your business's risk management vulnerabilities!)

Once the answers start coming in, Marcus could rely on a legal chatbot to familiarize himself with the compliance regulations of the mining industry. During his workshop, he could even use the chatbot tool to answer questions from his audience on the fly!

Legal chatbots are a great example of the approachability of artificial intelligence. Before AI, small business owners would have to weigh the pros and cons of consulting a lawyer (for a hefty hourly fee) or risking a potential legal vulnerability. Now, with legal chatbots, you can ask as many questions as you want, allowing you to be informed whether or not you choose to meet with a human lawyer.

FINAL THOUGHTS ON RISK MANAGEMENT

For small businesses, risk management issues aren't an issue...until one day, they are. Being proactive about your cybersecurity and legal protections isn't optional; it's necessary so you can stay focused on growing your business with minimal obstacles.

Artificial intelligence brings efficiency and accuracy to risk management, from identifying risks to optimizing contracts. There are many tools out there that make this field accessible, and by the time this book is published, I bet there will be even more than what I've mentioned here.

Your business should bring you joy. Don't allow yourself to be sidetracked by the unexpected. You have enough of that already as an entrepreneur and business owner. Through artificial intelligence, you can confidently navigate uncertain territory, knowing that you'll be protected in worst-case scenarios.

Chapter 12

AI + R&D and Innovation

This book promised to give you practical applications for using AI in your small business. From sales and customer service to logistics and legal compliance, you now have an abundance of artificial intelligence tools with real-world examples of how to apply this technology to your organization. The world of AI moves *fast* (I'd argue it's one of the fastest-evolving technologies today), which is why I've done my best to focus on strategy, stories, and examples that will make you think, "I can do this!"

In this final chapter, I want you to be inspired to dream bigger than ever—and employ artificial intelligence as a thought partner, researcher, and integrator to make an idea a reality. At the core of artificial intelligence is technology that merges human intelligence with computer systems, and its role as a catalyst for innovation can be colossal for businesses.

INNOVATING AS A SMALL BUSINESS

Artificial intelligence makes it possible to push the boundaries of every facet of your business. Its lightning-speed processing capabilities and ability to identify patterns can be a sounding board and trusted voice to explore "what if?"

Innovating isn't just about creating a revolutionary product or business vertical. It's about doing this differently, with your existing business functioning as your yardstick, as you continue improving in all areas. That's why this chapter will include some motivating examples of ways you can innovate in your business with artificial intelligence—whether it's the research you conduct, the website content you create, shopping experience in your store, or other business aspects that often get overlooked for the next shiny object.

Assist with Research and Development

What AI can do: Review data to quickly uncover patterns, observations, and ideas.

Recommended AI tools for this task: IBM Watson, TensorFlow, Google Cloud's AutoML

Data you might need on hand: Raw data, data schemas, metadata, performance metrics

If you task a team member with researching and developing a new business offering, how many days do you think they would need for the assignment? A week? A month? With artificial intelligence, you could split that time in half—and have a better output.

When you use AI for your research efforts, its vast data analysis capabilities can uncover patterns, observations, and ideas much faster than a traditional researcher would. You'll efficiently receive information about competitors, industries, customer challenges, and more, further freeing up your team to make decisions and go after that idea.

We reviewed AI's financial scenario planning capabilities in Chapter 7, but, excitingly, this technology also applies to research and development. Artificial intelligence can give you an objective analysis of the viability of a new product or service offering with various conditions. Want to know if your product would sell in an economic downturn? What happens if there are new environmental regulations? Got a good deal on an ingredient and wondering what would happen if the supplier went out of business? With AI, you can anticipate nearly every "what if?" and use the predictions to guide your product or service development.

For this type of modeling, IBM Watson and TensorFlow both have learning frameworks that decipher complex data, helping you seamlessly inform your research and development process. You could also check out an automated machine learning (AutoML) platform, like Google Cloud's AutoML; these user-friendly tools can help you create a model specific to your company's needs.

Innovate Your Website Content

What AI can do: Maximize business opportunities by improving your website content.

Recommended AI tools for this task: Adobe Express, NeuronWriter

Data you might need on hand: Existing website content (pages and blog posts), keyword data, audience insights, competitive analysis

Innovating with artificial intelligence isn't only about the products you create—it applies to your content as well. The keywords you utilize for your content help your ideal customers discover you. If you want to build organic authority for your business or your latest product, you're going to need to create content.

With artificial intelligence, you no longer have to spin your wheels to create valuable website or blog content. Artificial intelligence can be leveraged to explore new creative directions and uncover innovative content ideas that resonate. Your business can always be dynamic and forward-thinking with AI as a thought partner. Enlisting artificial intelligence's generative capabilities can help you create content of higher quality and volume, helping your business maximize opportunities for exposure online. The more high-quality and innovative content you create, the higher your site will be ranked by search engines, and the more visitors your site will attract.

AI in Practice

My clients Mary and Sean of Vindulge are food bloggers based in Oregon. Mary is a sommelier, Sean is a grill master, and together, they create incredible barbecue recipes with wine and champagne insights.

Vindulge has existed for years, and to be honest, it can be tough to stay inspired when they've created hundreds (if not thousands) of recipes. The burden of brainstorming (and even writing) is lifted through artificial intelligence when instead of being a copywriter, Mary can focus on being an editor-in-chief, directing artificial intelligence to create innovative content aligned with her vision for Vindulge.

Generative AI can create original ideas or new twists on existing ideas, acting as a partner in ideation. For example, Vindulge could share their most popular recipe names with a generative AI tool and ask for five to ten variations. The generative AI tool might even create a new version of a recipe if provided with the original instructions. Of course, Mary and Sean need to test out the AI-created recipes and provide their own human twist, but this could save them hours of time.

For your business's site, look at your most popular content and ask artificial intelligence to create similar or related angles for inspiration on what might land with your audience. Or ask artificial intelligence, based on trends, what auxiliary topics you should create based on what's performed well in the past.

AI in Action

Try a variation of this prompt:

 I am the creator of a popular barbecue blog called Vindulge. Our most popular recipe is Smoked Ham with Brown Sugar Glaze. Please come up with ten twists on this recipe that are SEO optimized. You can explore different flavors and cooking techniques, but I want the recipe suggestions to be similar to the original.

Creating twists on your popular Smoked Ham with Brown Sugar Glaze recipe sounds like a great way to keep your content fresh and appealing. Here are ten variations that maintain the essence of your original recipe while offering new flavors and techniques:

1. **Maple Mustard Smoked Ham:** Replace brown sugar with maple syrup and add a touch of Dijon mustard for a tangy, sweet glaze. This combination is perfect for those who love the classic sweet and savory flavor profile.

2. **Spiced Apple Cider Glazed Ham:** Use apple cider as the base for your glaze, adding cinnamon, nutmeg, and a bit of brown sugar. This version is ideal for autumn-themed posts or holiday cooking.

3. **Cherry Chipotle Smoked Ham:** Add a smoky, spicy kick by blending cherry preserves with chipotle peppers in adobo sauce. This recipe can attract readers looking for a bold, flavorful twist.

4. **Honey and Bourbon Glazed Ham:** Mix honey with a splash of bourbon for a deep, rich glaze. This combination can appeal to those who enjoy gourmet, adult-flavored twists.

5. **Citrus and Herb Smoked Ham:** Use a blend of orange and lemon zest with rosemary and thyme for a fresh, aromatic glaze. This lighter, brighter variation is great for spring and summer barbecues.

6. **Peach and Ginger Glazed Ham:** A sweet and spicy glaze made with peach preserves and fresh ginger. This can be a hit for those who enjoy fruity and zesty flavors.

7. **Coffee and Brown Sugar Crusted Ham:** Incorporate finely ground coffee into your brown sugar glaze for a rich, earthy crust. Perfect for coffee enthusiasts and a unique angle for your blog.

8. **Smoked Ham with Balsamic Fig Glaze:** Combine balsamic vinegar and fig preserves for a sophisticated, sweet, and tangy glaze. This can attract readers who are into artisanal or gourmet cooking.

9. **Caramelized Onion and Whiskey Glazed Ham:** Slow-cook onions until caramelized and mix with a splash of whiskey for a deep, savory-sweet glaze. This is great for readers who love a robust flavor profile.

10. **Asian-Inspired Hoisin and Honey Glazed Ham:** Use hoisin sauce, honey, and a touch of soy sauce for an Asian twist on your classic recipe. This can appeal to those looking for international flavors in traditional dishes.

Each of these variations can be optimized for SEO by using keywords like "unique smoked ham recipe," "gourmet ham glaze," or "easy holiday ham." Additionally, integrating popular cooking methods, seasonal ingredients, or trending flavors can boost your SEO efforts.

Preferred Platforms for Creating Website Content

Try these platforms for building websites:

- **Adobe Express.** When you're creating website content, don't forget to use Adobe Express for easy, innovative website graphics. Its features, like "Rewrite" for text and customizable templates, make it simple to create engaging visuals. By leveraging Adobe Express's AI tools, you can quickly produce graphics that are both professional and unique, eliminating the need to source constant new photography. This allows for personalized and versatile design, streamlining the creative process and helping your site stand out.

- **Adobe Firefly.** When creating visual content, use Adobe Firefly for image creation and ideation. Its "Text to Image" feature can produce unique images from text prompts, allowing specification of style and composition to craft a perfect look, reducing the need for additional photography. Integrated into Adobe tools like Adobe Express, Firefly generates tailored images, including photos, art, or graphics, for direct use in designs or as templates. Crucially, Adobe Firefly supports the Content Authenticity Initiative (CAI), creating commercially safe, traceable content that lets small businesses confidently use AI-generated images without legal concerns. This AI-driven approach fosters more creativity, experimentation, and innovation.

Consider Dynamic Pricing

What AI can do: Help you decide on dynamic pricing models based on historical data and economic trends.

Recommended AI tools for this task: Wiser

Data you might need on hand: Competitor pricing, market demand, customer behavior data

If you want to foster continuous innovation in your business's pricing strategy, you should explore dynamic pricing. (Don't you love how artificial intelligence can answer formerly daunting questions like, "How much should I sell my product or service for?") Dynamic pricing is the adjusting of your pricing strategy for different geographic markets, outpricing competitors, and maximizing the purchasing power of every visitor on your website. While all small business owners have systems to determine their prices (some might prefer intricate calculations, others prefer instinct), nothing quite compares to having artificial intelligence's savvy observations recommend pricing.

AI in Practice

Here is an example via my client and Brandmasters member Chandresh Bhardwaj. As a seventh-generation spiritual healer, Chandresh has a unique perspective on spirituality that fuses ancient wisdom with modern sensibility. He founded an online spirituality brand called Leela Gurukul, which helps seekers deepen their spiritual journeys beyond traditional "entry-level" meditation apps.

A few things to know about Leela Gurukul and Chandresh:

- The websites have two self-paced online courses for sale
- Chandresh also offers 1:1 spiritual coaching sessions, available as a digital product on his website

If Chandresh utilizes a tool like Wiser on his website, he'll have AI-powered dynamic pricing capabilities to optimize the prices of his digital courses and 1:1 coaching sessions in real time. Wiser's platform can:

- Analyze competitor pricing, market demand, and customer behavior to adjust prices dynamically.
- Implement price changes based on predefined rules and market conditions to maximize revenue and competitiveness.
- Provide recommendations for optimal pricing strategies, ensuring that the prices reflect current market conditions and maximize sales potential.

With Wiser, Chandresh can ensure that his pricing strategies are always competitive and aligned with market trends, ultimately helping him maximize the profitability of his digital products and services.

Improve Your In-Store Experience

What AI can do: Suggest ideas on how to adjust your store's layout, design, or traffic flow to enhance the customer's experience.

Recommended AI tools for this task: ChatGPT

Data you might need on hand: Store layout and design data, customer behavior data, sales and transaction data (but avoid uploading sensitive data to ChatGPT)

AI can accelerate your business's quest for innovation, even at the in-store level. The opportunities to improve and innovate brick-and-mortar stores through artificial intelligence are thrilling, to say the least. By leveraging artificial intelligence technology, you can free up your staff's time to focus on what matters most: meaningfully connecting with your customers in a personalized, engaging, and efficient shopping experience.

As mentioned previously, it best to implement artificial intelligence into your business gradually—and this particularly applies to the in-store experience. Since your initial app implementation will directly impact customers' experiences, making this adoption slow and intentional is essential.

Before we get to some in-store ideas, take a moment to brainstorm with your preferred generative AI tool. I promise this is a fun and rewarding exercise! The next time you're working in your store, take some time to observe and answer the following questions:

- **What is the in-store journey of the average customer?** Pay attention to how customers navigate throughout the store from start to finish. Where do they go? What do they buy, if anything at all? Who do they speak with? Consider (discreetly) making notes about individual customers over the course of an afternoon to zoom in on all the behavioral details of how and whether or not they make a purchase.

- **Where do your customers make slow decisions?** Is there a particular aisle where your customer is spending a lot of time? For example, if you own a convenience store, perhaps your customer spends ample time reviewing various soft drinks in your beverages section.
- **Where do your customers make quick decisions?** For your customers who quickly come in and out of your store, what are they purchasing? Is it something behind the counter where there's a sales associate talking up the product? Is the purchase always a particular item? Is there a guiding sign or piece of marketing associated with whatever they purchased? No detail is too small here, and all these clues will add up to a detailed picture for AI.
- **When do customers appear frustrated?** Hint: Spend extra time in your checkout area for this one. If someone is huffing while waiting in line, you might be able to leverage artificial intelligence technology with this down the road. I also recommend asking staff to (honestly) share any recent instances of disgruntled customers.
- **What types of questions do customers ask your staff?** Do they want help locating a particular product? Are they confused between two different options? Are they unsure about parking? Ask your staff to document all questions they receive on a given day, even the "obvious" ones.
- **How do customers interact with signs and displays?** This seems like a simple question, but there are multiple complexities to consider. First, note if your customers interact or glance at your signage *at all*. If they interact with your signs, do they act based on what the sign advertises?
- **What is the traffic flow in your store?** Do customers flow from left to right? Are they zigzagging? Where do they line up at the counter? All these details will help artificial intelligence potentially improve the store experience—and help you sell more product.
- **What are your most popular items?** Are there any products you can't keep in stock? Or products where you make the most margin? If you have data on *who* purchases these items, even better. AI can help you sell more of what is selling.

Remember: All the homework here does not have to be paragraphs long. Even bulleted points will do. The key is to give the AI tool all the information, even if some data is unclear. For example, if you note that every customer has a different flow in your store, that might be an opportunity for a potential new floor layout in the eyes of AI.

Here's an example of how you can give this information to your preferred AI tool to guide your next steps.

AI in Action

Try a variation of this prompt:

 I run a small convenience store in Columbus, Ohio, and I want to incorporate AI technology to improve the in-store experience. I am overwhelmed by AI and want you to provide me with a prioritized list of what tools I should use, in order, based on the following information.

In-store journey of the average customer:

- The average customer spends 17 minutes in my store.
- They usually go straight to the beverages section, which is on the far back wall.
- Sometimes people will pick up a snack afterward.
- Most interactions with staff are to get something from behind the counter, like cigarettes or lottery tickets.

Slow decision areas:

- Customers spend a lot of time in the specialty drink and energy drink areas trying to make a choice by reading labels.

Quick decision areas:

- People usually quickly add on gum to their purchase, which is located right at the checkout counter.
- We have a "deal of the day" for different snacks (displayed right upon entry), and that seems to be effective.
- We don't have any other marketing signage in the store.

Frustration areas:

- Customers get frustrated when there is a long line at the checkout counter, usually in the afternoons.
- Customers also get frustrated if their favorite beer brand (Heineken) is out of stock.

Common questions to staff:

- Locations for specific items. ("Do you have milk?")
- Price checks. ("How much is this?")
- Requests for items behind the counter. ("Can I please get a lottery ticket?")

Traffic flow in store:

- Customers tend to circle the aisles in a clockwise pattern, starting on the left side of the store. The checkout counter is near the right side.

Most popular items:

- High demand: bottled water, energy drinks, and local craft beers.
- High margin: snack foods like chips.

Feel free to ask me brief questions if you need more information before providing a prioritized list of AI tools for my small business. I plan to implement each app one at a time, and I want to start with what will lead to the most business results.

Let's say you feed this information into generative AI like ChatGPT. It will most likely provide a detailed list of ideas. It doesn't have to stop there. I encourage you to continue iterating your prompts and input like you might in a conversation, using ChatGPT (in this case) as a thought partner. Part of generative AI's brilliance is its ability to dive into any topic with absolute detail. Use this to your advantage. You don't have to be on this journey alone.

Network More Effectively

What AI can do: Review lists of people to identify and connect with potential networking partners.

Recommended AI tools for this task: OpenAI Playground

Data you might need on hand: Contact list, professional background information, interaction history, networking goals, event information, company information

Yes, you can use artificial intelligence to innovate the way you network too! Throughout this book, I've emphasized how artificial intelligence technology is a tool that helps humans do what they do best: connect with others. Whether you're researching for a new product, scoping out competitors, or wanting to maximize a meeting with a potential investor, artificial intelligence can do the heavy lifting of research so you can focus on the in-person experience.

AI in Practice

I have a fun example from my friend Mike Russell, AI content creator and founder of Music Radio Creative. His company provides custom voice-overs, radio jingles, podcast intros, and DJ drops, and, being in the music industry, making connections can be pivotal for getting ahead. Mike was scheduled to attend a large conference, and he was overwhelmed by the exhibitors in attendance. The conference was only a few days long, and he needed help identifying and connecting with the most relevant vendors to his goals. Here's how Mike used artificial intelligence to help him plan:

1. **Compiling a comprehensive list of exhibitors.** Mike used the ChatGPT API within the OpenAI Playground, which allowed him to request a script that scraped the names and competitors of all exhibitors from the conference's website. He received a list in CSV format shortly after running the script.

2. **Rating the exhibitors based on goals.** Once Mike had the CSV file with exhibitor data, he used ChatGPT's API once more to write a Python script. (This is advanced stuff, but interesting nonetheless!) He had the script rate each exhibitor out of ten based on alignment with his profile—a YouTuber, podcaster, business owner, and avid user of very specific audio tools—and goals. Once the script was done, he had a precise and prioritized list of exhibitors to meet with.

3. **Contacting exhibitors in advance.** Now with a prioritized vendor list in hand, Mike used LinkedIn Sales Navigator to find top contacts at each of the vendors. With the help of ChatGPT, he crafted brief personalized introductory messages, tailored to each individual, with the intent of meeting at the conference. He offered Google Calendar's scheduling feature as a way for these contacts to book appointments directly based on his availability.

This story is a methodical example of how to use artificial intelligence to innovate standard business conduct. Instead of meandering from vendor to vendor, ChatGPT helped Mike identify, connect, and meet with key contacts, maximizing his time at the conference.

Perform Project Management Tasks

What AI can do: Provide well-defined project management services.

Recommended AI tools for this task: Monday.com, Adobe Acrobat AI Assistant, Motion, Text Blaze, AudioPen

Data you might need on hand: Project details, task information, team information, resource data

I believe that innovation involves creating a culture of continuous improvement, and you can't improve unless you follow through with your ideas. Artificial intelligence comes with no shortage of ideas, but the way you will truly grow and thrive as a business is by bringing those ideas to fruition.

That's why I like using AI tools for planning and project management. In the Undefining Motherhood example I shared in Chapter 4, I gave an example of follow-up questions to help ChatGPT flesh out a detailed production plan for Katy's trade show appearance.

Preferred AI-Enhanced Platforms for Productivity and Project Management

If you're looking for an even more hands-on artificial intelligence experience, here are some tools to try out:

- **Adobe Acrobat AI Assistant.** Adobe Acrobat's AI features offer rapid insights and generative summaries, making it easy to digest and utilize key information. Notably, the AI Assistant minimizes the risk of hallucinations by pulling information exclusively from within the document, ensuring you get reliable outputs every time.
- **Monday.com.** Monday.com is my project management tool of choice for integrating AI to enhance task management. It uses

AI to intelligently assist with task allocation, helping you to efficiently organize and prioritize your workflow.

- **Motion.** This is the final project management tool I'll recommend. Motion positions itself as an AI-driven assistant that not only plans but also time-blocks your day based on tasks and priorities. Although I don't use it personally, I have friends who do and swear by its effectiveness.

- **Text Blaze.** While Text Blaze isn't an AI platform per se, it serves as the perfect complement to your AI workflow. It functions as a Chrome Extension for auto-text, allowing you to insert snippets, templates, and macros within Google Chrome. Any text that I find myself repeating in a browser—such as email copy or AI prompts—I aim to store within this tool for quick recall or to share with my team. I can easily do this using a text shortcut that I set, which allows for easy insertion with just a few keystrokes. Text Blaze also helps streamline communication and documentation, making it an effective tool for planning repetitive tasks or organizing project-related templates, ensuring consistency and saving time across your projects.

- **AudioPen.** AudioPen efficiently captures and refines spoken ideas by transcribing your voice and using AI to improve clarity and precision. It quickly converts thoughts into clear, actionable content, turning spoken notes into structured outlines or task lists.

- **OpenAI Playground.** OpenAI Playground lets users interact with the latest AI models to automate tasks like data analysis and text generation. For networking, it can be used to analyze lists of contacts or event attendees, helping to identify key individuals who align with specific goals.

With these tools, you can use artificial intelligence to streamline your workflow by capturing, refining, and organizing your ideas, which helps measure your project progress and goals. You'll be able to maximize the human resources you have at your disposal, ensuring their time is spent taking action. And with all of the automation tactics you've learned in this book, your team will be even more freed to focus on making your business the best it can be.

DEVELOPING A CUSTOM GPT MODEL

One of the final artificial intelligence features I'll leave with you is the ability to create a custom GPT. Essentially, any small business can customize its "own" generative AI program that's been pretrained for your organization's specific needs. Instead of starting a new Gemini or ChatGPT chat from scratch, where you must give paragraphs' worth of background, you can create GPT that is trained with information specific to your organization.

From an innovation standpoint, you can imagine how this would help with ideation, research, and information about your company. The GPT could be trained to be a brainstorming partner that's already been debriefed on conclusions your company has reached, products you already offer, and other details.

From a communications standpoint, your GPT could double up as a team member, giving real-time knowledge and feedback to clients or customers. My client J3P Health could create a custom GPT specifically for healthcare leadership. As the premier leadership advisory firm for the world's best-known healthcare organizations, J3P Health has unique insights on personal and professional development within healthcare. Their custom GPT could be tailored to support medical professionals between coaching sessions, thereby getting the "J3P Health experience" without requiring a meeting.

I do need to underscore that customizing your own GPT is a large undertaking. The system needs an immense amount of information to be successful, and you might need to partner with an AI development firm to get the GPT to a place you want. However, this could be a major competitive advantage for certain small businesses.

NOW IT'S TIME TO EMPLOY AI

Artificial intelligence can help you achieve your dreams. I say this from experience. Thanks to AI, I have a business vertical where I share artificial intelligence tools on social media and with members of my Brandmasters community, and, as a result, I got the opportunity to write the very book you hold in your hands. In the very early stages of writing this book (which, yes, I did write myself!), I knew I wanted to provide a practical and motivating take on artificial intelligence, complete with stories of real people using AI to create a life they love. My hope is that this book is the nudge you need to get out of your own way, fix what's holding you back, and take your business to new heights—with AI right by your side.

Index

Beyond the Book

Want a consolidated list of every tool mentioned in this book? Visit https://philp.al/200-tools for a list of the latest and best artificial intelligence tools for small businesses—tried and tested by yours truly. The list contains over 250 examples for a variety of business functions, including:

- Sales
- Marketing
- Social media and content creation
- Customer service
- Finance and accounting
- Operations and logistics
- Human resources and talent management
- Data analysis and decision-making
- Security and legal compliance
- Research and development and innovation

The best part? If any of the tools in this book rebrand or get acquired, my list will have the most up-to-date names and links to my recommendations, which means you'll spend less time googling and more time discovering how to implement this technology into your business.

For reviews and updates on technology and branding/marketing, you can also follow @philpallen on any popular social media platform.

About the Author

Phil Pallen is a brand strategist, keynote speaker, and content creator who helps professionals master their first impressions to grow successful businesses. Through his agency, Phil Pallen Collective, he's advised and designed over four hundred brands across thirty countries. He is a leading branding and online business expert with international media appearances on CNN, *Access Hollywood*, *Entertainment Tonight*, *Daily Mail*, and many others. Phil has delivered keynotes on five different continents; his nonconventional approach to personal branding and digital marketing has amassed a global audience.

Phil received his bachelor's degree in media, information, and technoculture from Western University. He also possesses a master's degree in entertainment business from Full Sail University. In 2022, Phil was inducted into Full Sail University's Hall of Fame to commemorate his professional accomplishments.

With a mission to empower small business owners with growth tactics and tools, Phil shares recommendations, strategies, and tools with his private membership community, Brandmasters, and with his audience of 200,000+ on social media.